A Nottinghamshire Christmas

A Nottinghamshire Christmas

Compiled by John Hudson

ALAN SUTTON PUBLISHING LIMITED

Nottinghamshire County Council
Leisure Services

First published in the United Kingdom in 1995
Alan Sutton Publishing Limited · Phoenix Mill · Far Thrupp
Stroud · Gloucestershire
in collaboration with
Nottinghamshire County Council
Leisure Services Department

British Library Cataloguing in Publication Data

A catalogue record for this book is available from the British Library.

ISBN 0-7509-0946-3

Cover illustration: detail from The Christmas Tree, *Albert Chevallier Tayler (Fine Art Photographs Ltd)*

Typeset in Garamond 12/13.
Typesetting and origination by
Alan Sutton Publishing Limited.
Printed in Great Britain by
Ebenezer Baylis, Worcester.

Contents

from

George, Memoirs of a Gentleman's Gentleman

NINA SLINGSBY SMITH

George Slingsby, born in 1889, was the son of a gardener at Babworth Hall, and at the age of fourteen he, too, entered into a life of service, rising from backstairs boy to footman at Welbeck, and finally as butler at Osberton Hall. His daughter Nina began to write about her father during the last years of his life – here recalling a Boxing Day hunt meet at which George, unwittingly but happily, proved the fox's greatest ally.

Squire Foljamb was a good master but a man of curious contradictions. He was justly proud of his widely-known wildlife sanctuary, and yet he rode to hounds at every possible opportunity and apparently spared no thought for the luckless fox, which almost invariably ended by being torn to shreds by a pack of fifty-two hounds. To George it was a nauseating sport, but servants were not supposed to hold opinions, let alone air them. The Squire owned a fine stable, and the family had been noted huntsmen from 1871, when Mr Frank

Foljamb had assumed mastership of the Burton hounds. After each meet there were dinners and hunt balls for the entertainment of the Squire's influential friends and followers of the hunt. The main staircase of Osberton Hall was lined with animals' heads, macabre trophies of previous kills. On such occasions, while carrying out his duties and mingling with the guests, George would often overhear a lurid description of the way in which their latest quarry had met its end; whether it had turned to make a last brave stand against impossible odds, or whether the poor creature had screamed in terror until the fangs of the hounds had silenced it for ever. George would leave the room feeling sick, and if those gathered there could have read his thoughts, he would not have remained as butler for long. It amazed him that these otherwise decent people could find such obvious joy in the suffering of any small creature.

Out with the Earl of Harrington's hounds at Oxton, *c.* 1910.

It was pure accident that George upset the important Boxing Day meet. About forty riders of both sexes were assembled at the front of the Hall, all bubbling over with excitement. The first whip was doing his best to control fifty-two extremely hungry hounds. Huntsmen might hotly deny it, but the hounds were kept on very short rations for several days before a hunt so that they would be keener to seek out the quarry and make a satisfactory kill. The opposite was the case with the huntsmen themselves, who sat on horseback while being served with hot refreshments before setting out. George, who led the procession of footmen outside, carried a huge butler tray laden with hot sausage rolls, thin toast spread with caviar, smoked salmon sandwiches, chicken pasties and stuffed olives. Immediately behind him, footmen carried the huge bowl of hot punch and large trays of crystal glasses. Hounds were milling around, sniffing at everything.

Seasonal greetings from Wollaton Hall, *c.* 1910, a focal point of county social life in Edwardian times.

As George approached the first rider, the lead dog got the scent of the piping hot tit-bits. That was all it needed to bring the whole pack hurling themselves at him in hungry determination.

Taken completely by surprise, George found himself flat on his back and the entire contents of the tray scattered over the ground. As he fell back he collided with the footmen behind him and they too went flying in an undignified heap among the fragments of broken glass. Seconds later there was not a crumb left; the hounds had scoffed the lot, including the stuffed olives. The first whip's efforts to muster them were unavailing. After this the fox could have sauntered by, dragging his brush, without being spotted.

Needless to say, there was no kill on that occasion, and although everyone present was terribly disappointed, they sportingly put it down to sheer bad luck. They made up for it by having a riotous time at the hunt ball later that evening. George was not held in any way responsible for the unfortunate incident and most people showed great concern until they were sure he was not hurt. He even came in for a lot of good-natured teasing during the evening's frolics.

Christmas in Florence, 1926

D. H. LAWRENCE

D.H. Lawrence, the great novelist born the son of a miner in Eastwood in 1885, spent his later years in the sunshine of Southern Europe. In this letter written to a childhood friend, Gertrude Cooper, some four years before his death, he comes over very much as the local boy made good.

Villa Mirenda, Florence
21 December, 1926

We are busy getting ready a Christmas tree for our peasants. There will be about twelve children, and I expect their parents will have to come to look. So many people work on this little estate. And the children are wild little things. They've never seen a Christmas tree, but they heard of some other English people who made one for the peasants, so they all had fits hoping we'd do one. We've got all kinds of wooden toys from Florence, and with a few glittering things and some sweets and dates, and the candles, it'll do for them. They never get sweets or anything like that from year's end to year's end. They're very much poorer than even the really poor in England. You see, there's no money. They just live on the wine and oil and corn and vegetables of the earth, and have no

wages, no cash, unless they manage to sell a barrel of wine. But this year there wasn't much.

Here, the peasants are supposed to do all the work on the land, and then they take half the produce, the landlord taking the other half. But when it's a little hilly estate like this, no pasture, no cattle, all just the hard labour of wine and a bit of wheat, a few vegetables and the olives, they don't come off very well. This bit of land round the villa has to support twenty-seven peasants, counting children. In England it wouldn't support seven. But we've no idea how poorly they live – like cattle. Still they are nice, and when we give them things, they always send us back a few dried grapes, or figs, or olives.

We shall give them their Christmas tree on Friday evening at sundown. And if the twenty-seven all of them come, it'll be like Ripley fair in this salotta. The men will have to have a glass of sweet wine, and a long cigar called a Toscana, and the women get a glass of wine and a few biscuits. There will be a buzz! I wish you could be here to help. But they talk such strong dialect that even when you know Italian you have a job to follow them.

Ada couldn't see the play *David* because Bertie was ill. I'm sorry, I should like her to have seen it, though I believe most of the people found it too gloomy. I think if it were being done again, I should alter the end and make it more cheerful. Myself, I hate miserable endings, now. But it's so long since I wrote that play.

A Christmas Party, 1900

OLD PAVIOR

This account of enforced but nevertheless genuine jollity at a school party in late Victorian times comes from the bicentenary book High Pavement Remembered, 1788–1988, *edited by the school's head of languages, Alan Bates. 'Old Pavior's' recollections first appeared in the Pavior school magazine of September 1955, when High Pavement School in Nottingham was still recognizable as the institution it was at the turn of the century. It is now a sixth-form college. I am just of that generation that can remember occasions such as this, having been fifteen in 1961; that, as Philip Larkin reminds us, was 'before the Beatles' first LP', and hence a time when shy boys and girls were still expected to dance holding on to one another, rather than simply gyrating on the dance floor two yards apart, as they were able to do a couple of years later. At least Old Pavior and his chums were able to break the ice quickly, to the extent that before long 'the fun was fast and furious'. Threescore years on, that phrase could never have been used to describe the scene when my single-sex grammar school came together with its sister establishment in nights of toe-curling embarrassment that remained strictly girls at one end of the hall, boys at the other.*

Many present-day scholars of High Pavement have enquired of the very old Paviors about the social activities of the old co-education school in the early 1890s. Was there anything to ameliorate the strict discipline and severe routine of school life? Education in the late Victorian or early Edwardian periods was a serious business, and was only concerned with hard and strenuous work based on the 'Three Rs'; no one had yet thought of developing school clubs or societies. Hence there were no literary, debating or science societies, and the social activities associated with these institutions in High Pavement today did not take place. It is true that we had a first-rate school concert with fine singing, and French and historical plays, which we did not understand but thoroughly enjoyed; but there was one outstanding social function, the memory of which is as vivid today as when it took place fifty years ago: the Christmas party for the junior school.

Somewhere about the beginning of December 1900 we were very surprised to receive a decorative card inviting us to a Grand Soiree in the School Hall to commence at 7 p.m. on 23 December, carriages at 10 p.m., RSVP. To receive such a formal invitation was indeed an occurrence we had not yet experienced – and what did RSVP mean, anyhow? Our knowledge of French was much more rudimentary than that of a present-day 1D pupil, but eventually we were enlightened, and having dutifully RSVPed by formal card, we purchased our tickets and eagerly awaited the night of the great event.

Oh, the preparations at home! We were washed and scrubbed mercilessly by our mothers, particularly behind the ears, and dressed in our 'Sunday best' with huge, white, starched linen Eton collars worn outside the coat and held in position by a white bow tie; above all, we had to wear white cotton gloves. We felt horrible. Then we awaited the greatest thrill of all, to ride in a 'growler', a four-wheeled horse-drawn

Enjoying a festive evening at Retford in the 1920s.

cab. These were generally used for funerals and weddings, but we understood that the elite were so conveyed to balls, dances and municipal functions. Usually, four boys who lived near to each other shared a 'growler', and when this drew up at the front door, the whole neighbourhood assembled to see the elegant young gentlemen of High Pavement. On our arrival at school we entered by the south or boys' entrance, and having presented our admission cards, we were given a wonderful programme with a pink pencil attached to enter the names of our dance partners. We were received and ushered into the hall by the second master, Mr J.B. Coleman, resplendent in evening dress, who announced each boy – 'Master Anthony Postlethwaite', or whatever – in turn.

The school hall was gaily decorated with festoons and Chinese lanterns and looked very beautiful. The girls were crowded together at the north end, and the boys were like a

flock of frightened sheep at the south end; although all the classes were mixed at the school, we were now all very shy and self-conscious. But we had reckoned without our master of ceremonies. There he stood in the middle of the hall, looking a fine figure in his immaculate evening dress, but with his tie always somewhat askew. Feared and respected by his staff and pupils alike, despotic and awe-inspiring, surely he was the last person to inspire happiness and to induce a convivial spirit of jollity to a party.

This was a new 'Daddy' Hugh, however; he was the embodiment of the Dickensian spirit of Christmas. He positively bounced about, laughing and joking and radiating good cheer. Like Mr Fezziwig, he was the life and soul of the party. He organised and supervised games – jolly miller, hunting we will go, musical chairs – and made us take our partners until all our gaucheries had disappeared and we were all mixed up laughing happily together. We even tried our feet at dancing – valses, polkas and the schottische – and got into a glorious mess, for very few could dance even a step. The fun was fast and furious, for after all, who cared? The headmaster smiled. The staff were equally helpful, and organised charades and acted amusing sketches; the head sang an operatic aria and Mr H.B. Tadman entertained us in his inimitable way with *When Father Laid a Carpet on the Stairs*.

And so on till about nine o'clock, when each boy had to select his girl partner for supper. This was not very difficult, for we knew all the girls in our own classes, and games and forfeits had produced some exciting episodes during the evening. My partner was what would be called today a redhead. Her name was Daisy Towle, and she was a most vivacious and attractive lass. However, this romance lasted only for one evening, and perhaps that was for the best for I, too, was a redhead. I have no doubt Daisy survived this episode and married happily; so to her and her children, if

they read this, I offer my felicitations. I have no doubt it will please her vastly to know that I have not forgotten her.

Having chosen our partners, or having had them forced upon us, we made our way through the beautiful rock gardens which existed on the site of the cycle sheds, and in the moonlight we could see the goldfish in the rock pools making goggle-eyes at us as we went to Stanley Road Preparatory School. Here, in the hall and the adjacent rooms, were beautifully decorated tables loaded with all kinds of comestibles to provide a gargantuan feast. There were stacks of sandwiches of all descriptions, jellies, blancmanges and dishes of fruit, heaps of cakes and pastries and gallons of tea. We fed sumptuously, for we were healthy mortals and such feasts did not often come during the year. Then crackers were pulled, mottoes read, marvellous reed instruments were played and everyone roared with laughter as the head put on his silly paper cap. Then came the climax of the evening, for suddenly there appeared in the doorway the figure of Father Christmas, whom we recognized instantly as Mr Pool. But we never let on that we knew; it would have been sheer sacrilege to have destroyed the Christmas tradition. Santa climbed up the ladder by the side of the enormous Christmas tree, alight with lanterns and loaded with presents for us all. The excitement was intense as we waited for our names, and we had great fun in unwrapping our presents and comparing our gifts – knives, toys, games, books, everything imaginable, but always just what we wanted.

Then reluctantly back to the hall for the final games and dance and 'goodnight', for it was 10 p.m. and our carriages awaited us. Then it was 'Home James' in the growler, and we were quickly hurried to bed – but not to sleep. What did it matter? There was no school for a fortnight, and that was indeed a blessing. To have returned immediately to the military discipline of the old school would have destroyed

forever the vision of the 'Spirit of Christmas Long Past' – Daddy 'Fezziwig' Hugh, all bouncy like Tigger in *Winnie the Pooh*, not that that splendid creature had yet been invented, and with a jolly, laughing face for once radiating happiness and goodwill.

Yes, our pleasures were very simple ones, and perhaps we did not realize that the party was in reality a lesson in etiquette and deportment for the young ladies and gentlemen of High Pavement. Happy days!

Snowstorm of Christmas Day, 1836

MRS A. GILBERT

Mrs Gilbert published her Recollections of Old Nottingham *in 1904, after captivating members of the Addison Street Church literary society with her stories of life in the 1830s and '40s a couple of years earlier. Her concluding reflection in this excerpt – to the effect that people in Edwardian times thought more of their play than their work – marks her as an astringent observer of local life, with a firm*

opinion on a wide variety of topics. 'You will observe that I speak of Nottingham as a town,' she notes at one point. 'The town and county of the town of Nottingham – a far greater distinction than the empty title of city.' Happily, she reflects here on a matter less controversial, a long-ago year when Christmas really was white.

The great snowstorm of Christmas Day, 1836, should now be mentioned. In that year, Christmas Day was on a Sunday. The snow had been falling since Wednesday night, almost without intermission. The roads in country districts were impassable, so that on Christmas Eve the different parishes sent out poor men by scores to open them. It is an ill wind that blows nobody any good; the families of these men rejoiced in that snowstorm, because of the excellent wages the shovellers received at a season when employment was scarce.

If the storm was severe in the Midlands, the records tell us how much worse it was in the south of London, where high ridges ran across the streets up to the first floor windows. For three days not a shop was opened, and intercourse between London and the South Coast was suspended for that period. My recollections corroborate much of this picture. On awaking that Christmas morn I gazed on the whitest of worlds; the snow was more than a yard thick, for it was up to the window sills; the horses were snowed up in the stable; silence reigned impressively supreme over the deserted streets; and the church bells themselves found no tongue to salute the happy morn. As the snow was still falling the ridges deepened, and so did the difficulty of getting to the animals. After hours of shovelling on the part of two or three of the household the stable at last became accessible.

The mention of Christmas recalls the paucity of holidays in those times – the only recognized public holidays being Sunday, Christmas Day, and Good Friday. I do not say that

Nothing moving today: big snows in Retford, *c.* 1920.

Saint Monday was not frequently observed, yet not as it is today. There were no Bank holidays widened out as now into a third of the week; no week's holiday for a workman in the autumn, no fortnight for his master; no Thursday or Saturday afternoons. The pendulum has swung to my thinking too much the other way, and people nowadays seem more intent on their play than on their working hours.

The 'Saint Monday' above was a phrase used throughout the Midlands and North for an unofficial day off after Sunday. It stems, jokingly, from the time when every single holiday was a 'holy day'.

from

Two of Clubs

JOAN WALLACE

Nowhere has the nightclub and pub life of Nottingham in the Swinging Sixties been more vividly and colourfully recalled than in Joan Wallace's Two of Clubs, *which tells the story of a popular 'sister act'. The narrator, Helen, and all but one of the characters are fictitious – but as Joan spent twenty-five years singing around the town, there is no doubting the authenticity of the book's racy flavour.*

On the day of the party I stayed in bed until lunchtime. Then I had a meal and caught the bus to Rita's flat. We rehearsed the harmony to a few Christmas carols, and as we did so I felt the hairs in the nape of my neck stand on end. I enjoyed singing the carols with Rita so much; derived a tremendous amount of satisfaction from the lovely sound we were both making. How fortunate we were, I thought, that next year we were going to earn our living doing something we thoroughly enjoyed. That is if Rita stayed with the act, of course, and didn't decide to go solo.

That evening the booking went very well. The audience were in a frivolous, free-spending mood because of Christmas. They were rowdy but it was a happy, festive kind of rowdiness. They joined in all the carols and clapped our other songs until their hands must have ached. Bottles of Guinness were sent over to our table faster than shells on the front line. By the time Neville arrived at the pub we were well and truly tipsy.

The young, unattached men bore down on us brandishing mistletoe. And married men got carried away with the spirit of Christmas when their wives left the room to go to the toilet – they, too, wanted a kiss from us. I proffered my cheek for the barrage of kisses, and so did Rita. She kissed away like mad, despite the presence of a now outraged and very jealous Neville. And to make matters much worse for Rita, half an hour before closing time, Jack Sargent and George The Hat walked into the room.

Rita caught sight of them and waved and beckoned them to our table. She introduced them to Neville, who forced a smile and said hello. George had a sprig of mistletoe pinned to his hat. I knew he was fond of his hat, I thought with some amusement, but decorating it up for Christmas was a bit much. Neville asked the two men to have a drink, and then made his way through the crowd towards the bar.

Sisters – Rita and Helen in Christmas spirit.

'I didn't think you'd turn up.' Rita leaned closer to Jack.

'I had to come and bring you a little bit of something for Christmas, Rita.' Jack felt in his inside jacket pocket. He handed her a small box which was decorated with a red satin bow. Rita slipped the box into her handbag and squeezed Jack's hand.

'Thank you, Jack. Neville's coming back from the bar. I'll look at it later.' She released his hand and sat up straight again.

George did not have much to say to me. After his unsuccessful journey back to my flat I could see that he was decidedly off me.

'We're going on to a party afterwards,' I told Jack. 'It's a sort of farewell party as well as a Christmas one. We're going to our boss's house, Ray Bowler from the Cresta Club. Do you know him?'

'Everybody's heard of Ray.' Jack sipped at his whisky. 'Got a finger in a lot of pies in this town. Good bloke, Ray is. I'll bet he gives fabulous parties.'

'Pity you can't come with us,' Neville butted in. 'But he's got a full house. We can't take anybody else.'

'Oh, that's all right, Neville,' Jack smiled at him. 'We've arranged to go to a party, anyway. Can't get round to them all, can we, George?'

'No, I'm about blotto now.' George blotted up more whisky.

'Oh, by the way,' Jack moved nearer to my chair. 'Would you like to do a couple of single spots at my clubs?'

I felt my heart jumping about. 'Yes, I'd love to, Jack.'

'Right then. Get your diary out, me duck, and we'll see what we can do.' He thumbed through the pages of a large red diary. 'Rita's on here and here – so can you do this one, and this one?'

I felt elated. This was like a Christmas present. All my doubts about Rita leaving the act were dispelled. I wanted to

hug and kiss Jack, he had made me feel so happy. So there wasn't anything sinister about him, after all. I wrote down the dates with trembling fingers. I didn't like going solo, but it would be good practice. I had to get used to singing on my own. Every pub and club couldn't afford a sister act.

I felt the magic sparkle return to my life and sat with a smile on my face that wouldn't go away. At the end of the evening we all stepped outside the pub. Rita, Neville and I talked to George and Jack for a while, then said our goodbyes and Merry Christmases. The sky was navy blue, and the glimmering stars reminded me of cut-out cardboard covered in gently vibrating tinsel.

from

Never Let Anyone Draw the Blinds

LOTTIE MARTIN

Sugar mice and pigs figure in the Christmas memories of Lottie Martin, who was born in Beeston on Good Friday, 1899, daughter of a foundry worker and fifth child in a family of seven.

Mason's Coffee Essence catches the festive spirit. An evocative advertisement from the Robert Opie Collection, Gloucester.

At Christmas we always hung our stockings on a line across the mantelpiece and everyone had a small present – an orange, an apple and perhaps a few sweets. My mother would always hang the kissing bush on the beam of the ceiling, and how we loved to see the sugar mice and pigs hung there! The kissing bush was only a big bunch of evergreen, and by the time Twelfth Night came along – when, according to tradition, all traces of Christmas festivities were removed – its twigs, along with the pigs, mice and paper garlands which festooned all the pictures, were full of dust and smoke.

We always had a tall lamp on the middle of the table, and my father would sit around making cork picture frames or drawing pictures of Ally Sloper, who was a character in the comic paper *Ally Sloper's Half Holiday*. There was a Sunday paper called *Illustrated Police Budget*, with horrible illustrations of women in blazing night attire, their hair flying and a caption along the lines of: 'Another Woman Burned to Death', or maybe the victims of this gruesome fate would be children. We were not supposed to see this paper, but as always, young ones have an uncanny delight in delving into forbidden territory. At other times my dad would make shadow pictures with his hands. How we loved this! Then my mother, as she sat working on the lace, would read the pictures in the fire, but our greatest delight was to hear her sing.

from

Victorian Worksop

MICHAEL J. JACKSON

This superbly detailed reconstruction of Christmas in Worksop in Victorian times comes from Michael Jackson's book, published by the Worksop Archaeological and Local Historical Society in 1992.

Although there were changes and innovations in the way it was celebrated, Christmas remained a time of general conviviality throughout Victorian times. For many, the focal point was the family gathering round the table to enjoy a special, often extravagant meal together. This remained constant; other activities and customs might alter, but they were merely trappings. No one, in 1837, would have a Christmas tree in their house. No one would send cards, yet by 1900 both were an integral part of the celebrations. Early in the reign, bands of mummers went their rounds, performing their traditional home-spun plays. As the queen grew older they became a rarity, and eventually died out. Carols that had long been favourites were heard less often, while newly written words and tunes gained in popularity. As is the way of things, some of the elderly regretted the changes. Others were less critical, and were just grateful for a day or two's break from the demands of work.

The run up to Christmas was far shorter than it is

nowadays. Although churchgoers were reminded of its approach by the Advent services, shopkeepers did not dress their windows and set out their seasonal displays until a week or so before the day. It was St Thomas's Day, 21 December, that really marked the beginning of the celebrations. 'Going a Thomasing' used to be quite common on this day, when it was customary for poorer people, particularly women and children, to call at the homes of their better-off neighbours seeking gifts of money or foodstuffs – oatmeal, potatoes, pieces of bacon, milk, eggs, currants, cheese, in fact whatever they might be offered. By the 1870s this practice was no more than a memory. 'I can remember the time when the whole female and child population of a village would turn out and beg from door to door of their better-off neighbours,' was one such recollection. Even after 'Thomasing' was no more, the day remained significant for certain of the poorest people, as it was the occasion when some of the town's charities were paid out. Following a short service in the Priory Church, the vicar distributed the bequests to those entitled to them. In 1884, upwards of two hundred people, mainly widows, received a few shillings each so that they might treat themselves to a little of the Christmas fare that was being set out in the shops.

A walk through the town three or four days before Christmas would see these displays at their best. Pride of place went to the butchers, as a prime joint was the first choice of many families for their festal dinner. Roast beef was the favourite, and the butchers boasted the pedigree and weight of the beasts they had bought from the recent stock markets. Pre-eminent was Mr David Winks, who in 1887 offered for sale four three-year-old polled Scotch bullocks and a heifer from the Worksop Manor estates, another Scottish beast from Welbeck, as well as two more heifers of more plebeian origin. Good supplies of mutton were also available, though pork was possibly the second most popular choice. For those who did

not kill their own pig, supplies abounded in the shops. Mr Schlor killed twenty-one pigs in 1875, weighing between seven and thirty-four stone each. That same year, Mr Palmer slaughtered seventeen, other butchers lesser numbers, while for many years in the second half of the century, no tea table was regarded as complete without one of Mr Nelson's celebrated pork pies in a prominent position on it.

By the 1880s, game and poultry were challenging the long-held supremacy of beef. Throughout the days before Christmas, dealers made the most ostentatious display in the town of their goods, virtually covering the frontages of their premises with their stock. Mr Lingard's shop on the Canal Bridge was completely hidden by 'a curtain of feathers'. Messrs Broadberry's establishment situated on the ground floor of the Town Hall was similarly festooned, and one day an observer noticed that, near by, 'wings were spread over a fair share of the market place'. As with the beef, so the game seemed to gain some extra desirability from its place of origin, and Messrs Lingard and the Broadberrys made special mention that their stock came from the estates of the Dukeries and from Osberton. Mr John Wright of Norfolk Street, a poultry dealer, took his goods to the customers, driving his sale cart to the four corners of the town. For those with money in pocket or purse the choice was limitless, while even for some of those less fortunate, seasonal benevolence provided a more limited share. One year, a Miss Sanderson paid for seventy-one joints of beef, between four and six pounds in weight, to be given to poor widows. Mrs Hodding gave a dozen slightly heavier pieces, and Miss Towers was likewise generous. These commissions were carried out by Mr Winks, and doubtless other butchers dealt with comparable gifts.

Even though shop windows tended to be small and multi-paned, dressing them was a widely practised skill. This was

especially so of the grocers, and of those in Worksop, that of Mr Leonard Towne, on the corner of Bridge Place with Watson Road, held first place. 'You should see Towne's shop,' was commonly heard among those indulging in the vicarious pleasures of window gazing. In 1887 he mounted a special display consisting of 'a glorious assortment of the chief materials which will go towards making plum pudding'. Other grocers were not far behind. Messrs William Allen, George Smith, W.J. Moore, James Valentine, Wortley Latham and Francis Hooson, all long established, decked their windows with seasonal fare to entice the potential customer from pavement to counter. The choice did not end there. At least eleven more grocers were in business in the town in 1887, as well as general dealers who sold groceries along with other things.

Drapers, chemists, stationers, booksellers and even furniture shops all vied for their share of the Christmas trade. The correspondent of the local paper who described their 1887 displays so effusively did imply, however, that a change was taking place in trading practices. Some shopkeepers were no longer sticking to their traditional lines of business, but were offering articles for sale hitherto associated with other types of shops. 'Drapers' windows nowadays do not include much in the way of real drapery,' he lamented. 'Still, there is some, and this year the draperies are half buried in curious collections of goods, which include work boxes and tooth picks, satin slippers and bonnet top knots, collars and cuffs and stockings, iron bedsteads and looking glasses, together with Christmas cards and presents and stationery generally.' As he was a stationer himself, the sight of the latter articles would particularly rankle with him. He later stated: 'The stationers and booksellers are one and all complaining that other traders are attacking them in most departments, and in fact stealing away their trade.'

Despite his feelings, he was able to say a few appreciative words about the displays of his fellow retailers. Of the drapers, he particularly mentioned Messrs Plant, Mr Walter Allen, Mr Middleton, Mr John Dougill, Mr Emblin, Mr Brooks, Mr Cooling and Mr Hodges. Though the nature of their goods did not lend itself to eye-catching displays, nevertheless the chemists had tried to make their windows neat and trim. Those of Messrs Marris, Jones, Baxter, Scaife, Fairweather and Mrs Pennington all met with his approval. Lastly, in his survey of the town's shops, he came to those in his line of business – 'the most important trades of all,' he wrote, casting aside all modesty. Messrs Sissons, Mr Robert White and presumably his own shop were all seasonally decorated – with Christmas cards, a recent innovation, featuring prominently.

Even for those with little money to spare, just to walk the gas-lit streets and gaze at these tantalizing displays was one of the pleasures of Christmas. This reached a climax on Christmas Eve, when such people were joined by those intent on last-minute shopping. For a few hours all was bustle and push. 'Butchers, bakers, grocers, drapers, tailors and stationers, one and all seemed to be up to the neck in business . . .' As the hours passed and twelve o'clock drew near, the crowds gradually thinned, the weary shopkeepers put up their shutters, counted their takings and thought about bed. Far from emptying completely, though, the streets continued to be astir, those going home being replaced by others wanting to see in the day on their feet, and by people coming out of the public houses. Some of the latter, usually groups of young men, 'set about making the night hideous' by attempting to sing well known carols and hymns. Greater harmony, however, prevailed at midnight, when in the Market Place the Worksop Brass Band struck up *Christians Awake!* They followed this with several other appropriate pieces before

marching to Victoria Square and repeating their programme. In 1887, the people who gathered there had been previously entertained by the St John's drum and fife band, which also performed at other parts of the town. At the same time, and reaching far and wide, the bells of the Priory Church rang out, heralding the great day. Some years earlier there was even more music. When in 1854 Mr Henry Wombwell's Quadrille Band played 'some most beautiful pieces in the principal streets', it was said to be reviving an ancient custom. Whether it continued in subsequent years probably depended on the weather and the contents of the collecting box.

Despite the late hour, lots of children were still about. While it was Christmas Eve they contented themselves with carol singing – usually badly, if the local paper can be believed: 'Their performances grow worse with each year . . . The girls are bad . . . but the lads are twenty times worse.' As soon as the bells and bands proclaimed the new day, they changed their ploy. For an hour or so they ranged through the town and at any house showing a light they paused and chanted all or part of:

> A wisher Merry Christmas
> An' a nappy New Year,
> A pocket full a' money an' a cellar full o' beer.
> A napple an' a pear,
> An' a plum and a cherry,
> An' a sup o' good ale,
> To make a man merry,
> A horse an' a gig, an' a good fat pig
> To serve yer all th' year.

This was followed by a loud knock on the door and the shouted request: 'Please will yer gimmy a Christmas box?' Weariness drove the youngsters to their beds by about one

o'clock, though some of them were on the streets again by seven, carrying on where they had left off a few hours earlier. Most appealed to seasonal generosity by using the above words, but there were some alternatives that were occasionally heard. Some proclaimed that:

We're all teetotallers
And don't want beer,

while others informed the occupants of the houses that:

I've got a little purse
Of stretching leather skin,

and that its capacity was at least equal to the penny that they hoped to receive. Now and then some youngsters, using the well known rhyme, called down blessings in the hope of a reward:

God bless the master of this house,
The mister-ess also,
An' all th' little children
That round the table go.

One jingle more common earlier in the century but little, if ever, heard towards its end, asked that the butler might bring out the ale, a crust and some mouldy cheese. The latter was a local product, much favoured at Christmas time and described as 'a ripe, rich farmer's cheese, moist and mouldy, the likes of which never comes nowadays into the market'. By nine o'clock the streets were quiet and remained so until people began to make their way to church or chapel.

Some of the older townspeople liked to think that these preliminaries to Christmas were more seemly and enjoyable in

A classic mumming group.

their younger days. By the 1870s tuneful Christmas singing was only occasionally heard, whereas thirty or forty years earlier more trained groups of singers and choirs seemed to be about. 'The waits we wait for in vain,' lamented one man in 1875, and a year later he elaborated further: 'Time was, a few years ago, when every choir in a town or village would turn out.' It was also customary for groups of lads and young men to perform traditional mummers' plays around the town. These too, according to the seemingly hard-to-please correspondent of the local paper, had sadly degenerated. In the middle years of the century upwards of half a dozen groups took their plays where they thought they might be welcome, and the householders generous. *St George* was the most popular of them, though *Th' Owd Tup* and *Poor Owd Hoss* were also performed. Each play began with a request that the actors might come into the house to entertain the occupants. In *St George*, a character called Betty Beelzebub spoke the opening words:

In come I that's never come before,
With my merry actors at the door.
Both merry act, dance and sing,
At your command they shall come in.

Once inside, the play began, each character first introducing himself:

In steps St George, the noble knight,
This noble champion bold.
With my bright sword and glittering spear,
I won three crowns of gold.

As the story proceeded, St George fought an evil character, at Worksop called Venture In, though in other places he was more generally known as Slasher or Slasher Knight. He was

wounded by St George, but miraculously cured by a doctor so that all ended happily. The plays made no claim to sophistication; they were a rumbustious assortment of vernacular speech, fighting, singing and dancing. At their conclusion, a collection was taken before the performers moved to their next venue. In some parts they were given on Plough Monday, though at Worksop they clearly formed part of the pre-Christmas activities. In the 1870s, just one troupe of mummers made its rounds, ignoring the private houses and concentrating on the public ones. By then the traditional words had been so altered as to be adjudged unfit for the delicate ear, and were described as 'a sad hashment of ribaldry and obscenity'. There was just one place where, for a few years, a more acceptable version of one of the old plays could be seen, and this was the workhouse. There the boys in residence had rehearsed what was variously described as 'The Peace (or Pace) Egg', which they performed in each of the wards of the house. This they did 'successfully and satisfactorily . . . in a manner that would put to shame most of those who go about our town with *Th' Owd Tup* and *Poor Owd Hoss.*'

About this time when mumming was declining and Christmas singing so inharmonious, another means was introduced of soliciting the odd copper. Two or more young girls carried from house to house a decorated basket or box which they simply called a Christmas. It contained a nicely dressed doll, a few packets of sweets and some small toys, the whole trimmed with ribbon, beads and shells. On admittance, the girls sang a carol, usually followed by *Jolly Wassail*, and then showed their Christmas to all present. Little is heard of this after 1880 so presumably it did not catch on, despite the approbation of the local paper.

Although many were late to bed on Christmas Eve, services at churches and chapels were well attended on the following

morning. All were attractively decorated with evergreens, plants and suitable texts. In 1873, those who formed the congregation at the Priory would see that 'the sanctuary was beautified with appropriate devices inserted in each panel of the reredos, in the centre being a large cross trimmed with holly. Plants were arranged on either side of the altar. The pulpit was festooned with wreaths of holly, and the text 'Peace on earth, good-will towards men', in white letters on a red ground, formed a fitting adornment for the centre.' These were doubtless admired by the large numbers who attended the fully choral eleven o'clock morning service, and the one in the evening. Although the usual Christmas hymns were enjoyed in 1887, many people were disappointed that the choir did not sing any carols. Perhaps the vicar felt that the way in which some of them were rendered in the streets on the previous night made them unsuitable for inclusion in divine worship.

For most, Christmas dinner was the highspot of the day, whether eaten in the villa of the well-to-do or the seasonally disguised grimness of the dining room of the workhouse. Roast beef was the widest favoured first course though other meats, game and poultry were enjoyed by some families. Afterwards, plum pudding was the universal choice. Over-indulgence was general. In fact, in some of the poorer homes, it may have been the only meal of the year where this was possible. Afterwards, when the table had been cleared, an hour or so by the fire was all that some desired. For those of more active inclinations, a walk, possibly up Sparken Hill, was a popular alternative. Christmas Day of 1879 was cold and frosty, and in the manner of Mr Pickwick, though with happier results, many people took to the ice. The Manor Lake, Beard's Dam and similar suitable venues were thronged with skaters throughout the remaining daylight hours. Some of the keenest even ignored the onset of the evening and continued

under the light of the moon. Although evening services were always well attended, and many people were content to remain indoors with their families, there were still plenty abroad on the streets; it was quite usual for them to be 'alive with persons for some hours'. Inevitably there was some noise and horse play, though this was not too prolonged, and by about eleven o'clock a general quietness pervaded the town.

Towards the end of the century Boxing Day, too, was regarded as a holiday, and many of the festive activities continued into it. Shops and works were closed, so there were plenty of people with time on their hands to wander the streets, greeting friends and, no doubt, taking refreshment at the inns. Those in quest of entertainment would usually find Worksop unrewarding, and some took the train to Sheffield, where the choice was greater. Had they remained in town, they would have had to have been content with the sound of an occasional group of singers or musicians, or even a belated glance of the mummers, all of whom still hoped to elicit the odd copper for their performances. Of organized activity, there was virtually nothing. In 1887 both the Primitive and the Free Methodists arranged a tea, the meal at the latter chapel being followed by a service of song. Otherwise, as a bystander noticed: 'Many people stood about or wandered about wondering what they should do next.' Things brightened up in the evening in many households, as it was party time, when friends gathered for a few convivial hours before work loomed again on the morrow.

Thus the year ran its course. As the cycle began again, people naturally wondered, perhaps with some apprehension, what the coming days would bring. This was especially so as the 1890s drew to their close, for not only did they mark the end of a century but, as many sensed, the imminent end of an era. The queen, old and frail, had not long to live. News of her death on 22 January, 1901 stunned Worksop. Most of its

townspeople had known no other sovereign. They could be forgiven if they thought that things would never be the same again. One who was certain of this was Dr John Eddison. Top hatted and frock coated, in the style of his younger days, he walked the streets of the town, shaking his head at the changes and innovations that had taken place. He was, however, in a minority. Most, though perhaps regretting some things that had been lost, looked approvingly on much that they saw, and felt that Worksop had emerged from Victorian times a much better place than it had been at their beginnings.

A Christmas Hamper, 1895

A couple of days before Christmas in 1895, J. Willatt and Co. of 17 Chapel Bar, Nottingham, was advertising what it called its Special Quality Hamper No. 3. This cost twenty-one shillings or a guinea – one pound and five pence in today's terms – and consisted of: One bottle, fine old Cognac brandy; One bottle, fine old Scotch or Irish whisky; One bottle, Nicholson's gin; One bottle, fine old port; One bottle, fine old sherry; and One bottle, Pomme et Fils special cuvée champagne. A hamper being just that, a strong wicker basket was obviously included in the deal.

The bustle of Market Place and Market Street, Nottingham, in the early years of this century.

To stock up with delights of this sort for around the price of half a pint of many of today's designer beers seems no bad idea – but, of course, there is always the other side of the story. Even as late as 1914, nearly twenty years on from Willatt's offer, railway porters were earning from a pound to twenty-six shillings a week, carters from twenty-four to twenty-seven shillings, bakers from twenty-eight to thirty-eight. Nottinghamshire miners were expected to settle for eight shillings and fivepence or around 42p a day – so they, along with the lace girls and the agricultural workers, were unlikely to be washing down their Christmas dinners with bubbling glasses of Pomme et Fils.

Christmas in the Trenches

These recollections are drawn from The Robin Hoods, 1914–18, *an account published in 1921 by officers of the 1/7th, 2/7th and 3/7th battalions of the Sherwood Foresters. The regiment began to be mobilized on 5 August 1914, the day after war was declared, spent the first Christmas of war training in Essex, and sailed for France, many of their number never to return, on 28 February 1915.*

Christmas 1915

The battalion remained at Boeseghem until 26 December, and during this period almost daily was engaged in route marches, march discipline being strictly enforced.

(25 December) Christmas Day – Christmas in France. Constantly during this day all Robin Hoods thought of their loved ones in England. In the early morning a large number attended communion service in the schools at Boeseghem, the service being taken by the brigade chaplain, the Rev. H.P. Hales. Afterwards, football matches and then Christmas dinner. Plum puddings had been sent to the battalion by the London *Daily Express*, and the battalion transport had the day before been sent to Aire, where officers purchased a number of other luxuries for their company dinners. The stress of the past ten months had knit all ranks very closely together, and old comrades who had given the great sacrifice were on this day, of all days, specially remembered. Can they ever be forgotten? What a band of brothers the Robin Hoods had grown to be. The *esprit-de-corps* in the battalion was wonderful; all ranks were bound together by danger, endurance and hardship, cheerfully borne in the days gone by, and the thought of the unknown future which lay before them.

The various companies of the battalion had their Christmas dinner served in the haylofts and other quarters in which they were billeted. In the evening, a concert was held in the largest room in the village, but unfortunately this could only accommodate a portion of the battalion.

(26 December) The Robin Hoods marched from Boeseghem to St Isbergues, where they were billeted in the vicinity of D'Aire La Basee Canal, and remained in these billets until 7 January, 1916, waiting for further orders to proceed to Egypt. During this period the battalion undertook several route marches with the brigade to surrounding

villages, Mazinghem, Rombly, Quernes. It was whilst the battalion was billeted in these quarters that it parted with its mascot, a black and white dog of the collie type. This dog was found in Ypres in June 1915, and attached himself to the Signallers, and accompanied the Robin Hoods on all their marches, always going with them into the trench line. He was known in the battalion as 'Bloody Wipers', but as the Robin Hoods were now under orders for Egypt, it was felt there would be difficulty in taking him overseas, so with great regret he was given to a Frenchman on one of the canal barges.

Christmas 1916

For weeks we had all been engaged in abstruse calculations to determine whether we should be 'out' or 'in' for Christmas, and we were fortunate in being 'out', though we relieved the Eighth Battalion again on Boxing Day. We had a good Christmas, despite weather and surroundings. It was celebrated by an absence of working parties, good dinners, and a smoking concert in the evening. Presents, too, were not wanting, notably a gift of a hundred cigarettes per man from Mr W.G. Player. We were glad to receive messages from many old friends, notably Colonel Brewill.

It is hard to write of this period without almost monotonous references to the weather. Indeed, it dominated everything, and the concurrent problems of trench feet and trench fever came to the fore from the first. By now, however, we had perfected an arrangement which was to prove almost entirely successful, and contributed perhaps more than anything else to the battalion's health and success throughout the winter. A large cellar at Battalion Headquarters in the line was converted into a drying room. Here were wire beds for twenty men, with a plentiful supply of blankets and dry clothes. Braziers were always burning, and stretcher bearers in

attendance. When in the line, every man was sent down there every day, where his feet were inspected, washed in warm water, and rubbed, and dry socks and gum boots issued to him. Any man showing signs of frost bite was detained for some hours, and allowed to sleep in warmth and shelter.

The labour and organization this involved were amply repaid, since for as long as it subsisted, only three or four men left the battalion with trench feet. It was also of incalculable value for patrols, who invariably returned exhausted and drenched to the skin. They were given a hot meal and enabled to sleep whilst their clothes dried, and returned to their companies the following afternoon ready for duty again. Another great boon were the Brigade Baths, which were established at Souastre. These were steam baths, and proved a remarkably effective way of utilising the scanty supplies of fuel.

We returned to the line on 26 December, and the next day were visited by Mr Philip Gibbs and the official photographer. It was a very amusing visit, and we were very glad of the excellent photographs which resulted – though had their visit been but a day or two later, Mr Gibbs would have found more stirring copy for his readers. The next morning at 3 a.m., under an intense barrage, the enemy attempted a raid. It was hardly big enough to ruffle the quietness of the Western Front in an official communique, but it was sufficiently serious for the troops who met it. It was a well conceived raid, for the enemy's barrage never quite lifted from our line. The isolated forward posts, taking what cover the battered trench afforded, noticed its weakening and saw the enemy already in our wire.

He appeared in great strength before our Lewis gun post, offering a splendid target. But the gun had been damaged in the barrage and the little party had to rely on their rifles. The fight was short and sharp. The enemy was repulsed, but not

before Lieutenant Barnes, who had taken command of the post, had fallen mortally wounded by a German bomb. In addition to this gallant officer we lost one man killed, two wounded and two missing. The fate of the two latter remained a mystery, but it was thought that they must have been either struck by shells or caught in an unoccupied portion of trench whilst passing from one post to another, and so captured. The occasion, however, did not pass without gaining an honour for the battalion, Lance Corporal Stringer, who was attached to the Brigade Stokes Mortar Battery, being subsequently awarded the Military Medal for his gallantry on this, as on many other occasions.

Relieved on 30 December, we returned to Fonquevillers and Souastre for a welcome rest, and found a draft of about a hundred reinforcements, of which we were greatly in need. These came from the Sherwood Rangers, and their splendid quality more than made up for their unfamiliarity with infantry drill – a deficiency which was very soon rectified. The two companies who had been at Fonquevillers for Christmas now held belated but very satisfactory festivities at Souastre; and so the New Year came in.

Christmas 1917

On Christmas morning, in fine frosty weather, the battalion moved off from hutments at Beaulincourt, and marched a distance of three miles to Bapaume, where it entrained for the railhead near Gouy-en-Ternois. The ordinary discomforts of a troop train, lacking heat (but not ventilation!), were enhanced considerably by the memories called up of Christmas warmth, food and cheer, and it was a very dispirited battalion which detrained in a heavy snowfall to face a seven-mile march after the interminable railway journey. The genius of the British soldier, however, can convert the most ramshackle of quarters into a 'home from home', and it did not take the men long to

settle down in comparative comfort in the billets which Gouy-en-Ternois provided. The population of the village had dwindled owing to the exigencies of the war, fifty-five out of its normal population of three hundred being away on service, and only the youths and old men remaining to 'carry on'.

Frost and snow continued for some considerable time, and very little hard training was done. The time was filled up by snow fighting, and what were meant to be football matches, but which the condition of the ground ruined from the point of view of skill. At this time an amusing and original competition was organized by the brigade, consisting of a four-mile run by companies. Every available man had to parade with his company, and the company commanders had to produce a parade state showing exactly how any absentees were employed. Marks were deducted for men who were not on parade, unless a satisfactory explanation of their absence was given, and each officer or man who completed the course within the prescribed time gained a mark for his company. The going was particularly hard, as the roads were covered with ice; hence it was no mean task to obtain a mark. However, the men enjoyed the life thoroughly, and the semi-relief from hard training was regretted by very few.

The snow at the time was very deep, and the battalion had to supply fatigue parties to dig out trains and stranded transport. These parties had to take rations for three days, and were often on duty for longer periods.

New Year's Eve was celebrated in fitting style, and the evening was concluded by saluting the departure of the Old Year by the sounding of the Last Post. At one minute past midnight Reveille was blown as a greeting to the New Year, which was ushered in with great hopes. It was little thought that before the year was ended, a successful peace would be concluded, or that the battalion would pass through such terrible times as in the March and April which were to follow.

Christmas, 1965

Ten things you have forgotten about the festive season of three decades ago:

1 Turkeys were four shillings (20p) per pound.

2 Hucknall Town railway station was about to close under Dr Beeching's axe – on 3 January 1966.

3 *My Fair Lady* was the big show at Nottingham Theatre Royal.

4 Some seventy-six people died nationally on the roads over the Christmas holiday, including a Hucknall woman killed in an accident at Calverton.

5 On Boxing Day, full-back Henry Newton scored the winning goal for Forest against Everton, in front of 34,750 at the City Ground; County won 3–0 at Tranmere, with goals from Denis Shiels, Ron Still and Dick Edwards.

6 *The Sound of Music* seemed to have been showing forever in the main auditorium at the Nottingham Odeon.

7 Max Bygraves, Nottingham's Leslie Crowther, Andy Williams, Jack Warner, Norman Vaughan, Terry Scott and Ken Dodd were some of the star names on BBC1 on Christmas Day – but the 8 p.m. peak hour spot went to an ancient Bob Hope and Bing Crosby movie, *Road to Bali*.

Christmas dinner is twice as festive with WINE!

Try it—and give your guests a treat to be remembered long after the holly has been taken down and New Year resolutions gone the way of broken dreams. May we make a few suggestions?

SOUP is all enchantment when partnered by a good sherry. We recommend **Vino de Pasto,** light, pale, not too dry (18/-). **Amontillado,** dry, pale, delicate (19/-). **Shooting Sherry,** pale, medium (19/-).

TURKEY or GOOSE. Noble birds gain in splendour when toasted in burgundy. Why not, inexpensively, try our **Beaujolais** (10/6d.) or our **Nuits St. Georges** (12/-). **Fleurie 1952** (23/9d.) adds a bouquet of flowers from Southern Burgundy, while the glorious **Chambertin 1949** (61/-) is fit for a king. Claret, too, is a lovely companion for your Christmas bird. We offer a capital range that starts with **Medoc** (8/6d.) and aspires to the fabulous **Chateau Haut Brion 1952** (45/3d.)

PLUM PUDDING. 'There's richness!' as Dickens said. And what nicer way to compliment the cook than with a dessert wine of harmonising bouquet. A choice **Sauternes** (11/6d.), say, or a full, sweet **Barsac** (12/-). A delicious but little-known alternative—**Muscat Vin de Liqueur** (10/3d.), a rich beauty from Frontignan. Or—to fill your table and your memory with fragrance—the rare **Chateau d'Yquem 1960** (33/9d.)

Some play it cool and start Christmas dinner as they mean to go on—with champagne. We can offer you all the famous brands plus a discovery of our own: the elegant **Roger Picot,** a honey of a wine at only 23/9d.

AFTER DINNER. For traditionalists, our **Hunting Port,** a distinguished tawny (18/-) makes a charming finale.

Whatever your choice this Christmas, you can indulge it to the full at:

SKINNER & ROOK

Wine Merchants of the City of Nottingham

VINTNERS YARD · CLUMBER STREET · NOTTINGHAM

Telephone Nottingham 44504

Rich fare, low prices – or so they seem today. The cost of high living in 1965.

Christmas Fayre

WILL BE AVAILABLE AT

THE VICTORIA HOTEL

from Monday, 6th December 1965

THE MENUS FOR BOTH LUNCHEON AND DINNER ARE AS FOLLOWS

LUNCHEON 22/6

Hors d'Oeuvres
Chilled Melon with Globe Ginger

Cream of Mushrooms

Roast Norfolk Turkey
Chipolata — Cranberry Sauce
Thyme and Parsley Stuffing
or
Roast Leg of Pork
Crab Apple Jelly — Onion Stuffing
Brussels Sprouts,
Roast and Creamed Potatoes

Christmas Pudding
Brandy Sauce
Mince Pies
Various Ices

DINNER 27/6

Hors D'Oeuvres
Hot Sherried Grapefruit

Beef Consomme Brunoise

Fillet of Sole Amiral

Roast Norfolk Turkey
Chipolata Sausage
Cranberry Sauce
Thyme and Parsley Stuffing
or
Roast Leg of Pork
Crab Apple Jelly
Onion Stuffing
Brussels Sprouts
Roast and Creamed Potatoes

Christmas Pudding
Brandy Sauce
Mince Pies
Various Ices

The usual extensive choice of Wines, for which the Victoria is noted will be available as usual

VICTORIA HOTEL

MILTON STREET · NOTTINGHAM

Telephone 48221 for Bookings

8 Nottingham clubs and pubs where you could twist the night away included the Union, the Beachcomber, the Boat, the Jazz Club, the Fifty-Nine, the Gallery, the Rhythm Club, the Parkside, the Dancing Slipper, the Calypso and Eve's. Scoop of the season, however, went to the Britannia Rowing Club, who had landed the super-cool group the Herd.

9 You could hire a nineteen-inch television for 7*s* 11*d* a week – less than 40p – at DER in Nottingham, Newark and Mansfield.

10 Some two thousand Scots and North-eastern miners who had been redeployed in the East Midlands coalfield ensured that most of the thirty-one Nottinghamshire and North Derbyshire pits took a day off for Hogmanay.

from

Georgian Southwell

Georgian Southwell*, edited by R.E. Hardstaff and Philip Lyth and financed by Newark and Sherwood District Council, draws on the journals of the George Hodgkinsons, attorneys at law, from 1770 to 1781. This excerpt is by George Junior, who worked irregular hours but often finished early enough in the day to be able to enjoy an active social life with 'our set', a well-to-do circle of clergy, professional men, landowners and military officers.*

Christmas and New Year were not public holidays at this time, but the diary entries for this period relate to pleasure more than usual, and if work did not cease, it certainly eased off. Christmas fare in 1781 was very similar to what is usual today, with the exception that oysters were included. There was turkey, game, leg of lamb, hare, with fresh pineapple and grapes grown in the local hothouses for dessert; sherry, port and madeira were wines the Hodgkinsons normally had in stock, punch was popular, and gin, and of course ale, all of which helped brighten the Christmas celebrations. The first two weeks of the New Year passed very agreeably.

1 January 1781

Mr D. Rastall sent me an invitation to attend an assembly tomorrow evening . . . Dined at the Palace with our family, adjourned to the evening prayers, after which drank tea and played Pope before supper . . . about eight, Mr Neale from Stamford, Miss Pierrepoint's intended, and Mr King (Rector of Uffington) came in totally unexpected, but very cordially received. Mr Neale sent us a fine hare and amongst conversation found out that he was the donor of the venison, oysters etc that we received since Miss Pierrepoint came here, which she pretended she never could inform us who was the donor. Spent a very merry evening and I sang several songs when we did not reach home till after one.

2 January

Returned home about half past three, dined at Mr Stenton's but returned soon after dinner when I found Mr Barrow [Reverend William] just arrived – Mr Neale and Mr King and Mr R. Barrow [school master, 1774–85] were also at our house (they had dined there) and who with Mr B adjourned into the office to play a rubber of whist. Drank tea at home . . .

adjourned to dress – and arrived at the Assembly Room about eight, where I found a very large and numerous meeting. I danced with Miss Pierrepoint and my sister Ann, with Mr Neale and Mr Masson with my other sister Su. We broke up about one, after a very entertaining though crowded dance; in short, the assembly was very brilliant and well conducted by Mr D. Rastall, but suspect it was paid for out of the public funds, as the King is out on a journey to Wirksworth in order to try and settle his affairs. Mr Neale and Mr King returned home with us to supper when we kept it up till between one and four.

The Assembly Rooms are now incorporated in the Saracen's Head Hotel, but the old entrance and portico can be seen from the street. Miss Pierrepoint was the daughter of a friend who lived at Uffington, near Stamford. She was visiting the Hodgkinsons and was the object of Mr Neale's attentions.The 'King' referred to, in addition to Mr King, was not George III but the person appointed to preside over the organized festivities for the season as master of ceremonies, for whom Mr Rastall was deputizing.

3 January

Received a barrel of oysters from Mr J. Truman and a turkey directed for Miss Pierrepoint. Adjourned to Mr Fowler's, where were Messrs Stenton and Law with whom I sat more than an hour and then adjourned to our Oyster Club.

4 January

Received a very fine quarter of lamb, which came directed for Miss Pierrepoint. Drank tea at home, after which called at the Palace when I invited 'em to dinner here tomorrow . . . supped at Mr Buggs.

5 January
Mr and Mrs Barrow and Mr W. Barrow dined with us and spent the evening, when we had a fine turkey for dinner and for supper a prodigious fine shoulder of lamb. Mr William Becher came to us in the afternoon, when we had a kind of concert before supper, after which we played loo, and after we had supped exerted ourselves in the vocal way and were as merry as wine, punch and good company could make us when we kept it up till near two. My sister's christening was to have been this evening, but some of the parties intended to have been invited were engaged, from which it is postponed till Monday without fail.

The Christmas Treadmill

BENJAMIN HUTCHINSON

What a charming Christmas present for the inmates of the Nottinghamshire House of Correction at Southwell in 1822 – a treadmill to call their very own. It was installed on 22 December and up and running by the next day. In the following year Benjamin Hutchinson, the prison surgeon, published his extremely pro-establishment views on the regime there, giving his thoughts on the treadmill in a user-friendly question and answer format.

Q When was the tread-mill established?

A 23 December 1822.

Q What number of men have been employed on an average?

A Daily average from 23 December 1822, to 17 September 1823, both days inclusive, 45.

Q What number of men are this day employed?

A Fifty.

Q What complaints have been made to you by any prisoner employed in this mode of discipline?

A None; not a single complaint.

The treadmill was admired more by the prison authorities than by the men who had to work it.

Q What accidents have happened to the men, and what to the machinery?

A One man had his foot slightly bruised, but this occurred through his own wilful neglect in coming off the wheel. No accident has happened to the machinery.

Q At what periods are the men relieved?

A One man gets off the wheel every minute, allowing each never less than one fourth rest, and occasionally nearly one-half, according to the number employed at each wheel. Thus, if twelve are employed at a wheel, nine are on the wheel and three off, which gives one fourth rest. If ten are employed at a wheel, seven are on the wheel and three off, which gives nearly one half rest, one man getting off, and one on, every minute.

Q In what periods do the wheels revolve?

A Two of the wheels on the ground floor make two revolutions in a minute; and the two wheels on the upper floor make three revolutions, while those on the ground floor make four.

1814: The Thirteen-week Frost

LEN MARKHAM

Weather patterns are confusing – sometimes our modern winters seem to offer conclusive proof of global warming, while at others we can believe those who tell us to expect a mini-ice age to dominate the meteorological picture for the rest of our lives. In the face of such prophets of gloom, we usually reflect that however bleak the prospects, we still have a long way to go before we are roasting oxen on our frozen rivers. We all know this happened in times past, largely through Dutch landscapes of the kind that find their way on to Christmas cards. But as Len Markham reflects in his 1994 publication The Derbyshire and Nottinghamshire Weather Book, *the Trent at Nottingham, on at least one occasion, was the scene of just such a remarkable spectacle.*

Beginning on Christmas Eve 1813, a straitjacket frost held Nottingham in its grip for thirteen weeks. Record low temperatures were experienced, the thermometer registering a numbing New Year low of minus seventeen degrees Centigrade at Lenton Priory on 14 January. The river Trent and local canals froze solid, and encased in thick ice, roads became all but impassable.

The novelty of walking on water and opportunities for

Cold as Christmas, but with little good cheer. Mansfield Road, Nottingham, in 1898.

skating encouraged local people to flock to the Trent. Bonfires were lit along the bankside between Trent Bridge and Wilford Ferry. Meals were cooked on the ice and one wit using the accumulated ice in Market Place even carved himself an icy pigsty fitted with a door and two prize sows! But chilly entertainments apart, it was an arduous time.

Hoots from *The Owl*

Scandal sheets were a familiar feature of late Victorian life, discussing the private lives of people prominent in the community they covered with a candour that was not seen again until the satire revival of the 1960s. Nottingham and district's penny dreadful of this kind was The Owl, *a constant thorn in the side of the pretentious, the lecherous, the power-hungry and the just plain boring. Its reporting, as a result, was not always a model of the temperate and impartial, but over its many years it raised a thousand laughs, wounded unfairly on occasions, but hit its target fairly and squarely more often than not. These stories from its issue of 4 January 1878, are typical – railing against the incompetence of the authorities, standing up for the little man and taking well-aimed swipes at narrow-minded civic dignitaries. What is the betting that the mean 'Another Billy' of Newark kept that belittling nickname in some circles in the town for the rest of his life?*

Bulwell Ducks at Selston

One Hucknall Torkardite at Christmas purchased a couple of ducks from a friend at Bulwell. His widowed mother, who lives at Selston, came to spend a few days with her son, and he gave his mother one of the ducks to take home with her. On getting back, a younger son proposed to keep it and not eat it. Another one was also purchased, and the lad, pleased with his

ducks, was eager to call the neighbours' attention to them. Next night the old woman was roused out of her bed, and getting down stairs, found her lad with the handcuffs already on his wrists. The police officer said they were wanted for some ducks which had been stolen. Despite explanations and entreaties, they were both taken to the Hucknall Police Station and locked up, while the ducks were taken to the farm from which some had been stolen for identification. The farmer said they were not his. Then the officer carried the ducks to Bulwell and interviewed the shopkeeper who sold them. He laughed and said: 'They are not mine, they were bought and paid for four days ago.' These zealous officers not having a particle of proof against the widow and her son, they were allowed to depart – another instance of the stupidity and bungling of the County Police.

A Christmas Funeral at Ruddington

Though it was Christmas Day, a funeral bell was tolling. An open grave yawned for the coffin containing the remains of Jesse Hickling. The funeral cortege passed from the church to the tomb, and the funeral ceremony having been finished, the clergyman went home to dine. The scene which ensued is too shocking for lengthened description. The grave is a narrow, narrow home at best, but poor Jesse Hickling's grave would not admit his coffin. The mourners stood in the bitter cold while the place of sepulchre was being enlarged. No fewer than five attempts were made to lower the coffin before it was laboriously squeezed to the bottom. By this time, three hours of mortal agony had elapsed – agony which only those who have been waiting mourners can in any measure understand! Who is responsible for this indecent outrage on the sanctity of sorrow?

The Newark Paupers Robbed of their Beer

A paltry cheeseparing crew must the majority of the Newark

Board of Guardians be. Why, they passed a resolution to deprive the aged inmates of the workhouse of the usual allowance of ale to their Christmas dinner. 'Another Billy' was the leader in this miserable movement. Strange so many Newark notables remarkable for their vagaries should be known by the name of Billy! 'Another Billy', however, is not the only instance of a man who has risen from bottle washing to brewing, oppressing the lowly class from whence he sprung. This much, nevertheless, may be said in extenuation: 'Another Billy' cannot claim to have much confidence in the article he manufactures, since by a solemn resolution he has affirmed that it is not fit for paupers to drink!

Beware of the Pit!

Councillor Trevitt was in the pit at the Theatre Royal on Saturday night and incontinently sloped when the villainous Blue Beard sang:

> . . . and Trevitt will be Alderman,
> When the world's turned upside-down.

It is scarcely the correct thing to spot so distinguished a member of the Corporation, when he has gone to the pit expressly that he might enjoy himself, as people of rank are often glad to do, incognito.

from

Life of a Country Boy, 1925–1940

VICTOR SMYTH

Victor Smyth grew up in the Newark area in the thirties, and has vivid memories of a pre-war town very different in spirit from the community of today.

Christmas was always a time of enjoyment for us children, a time when everyone was happy as they hurried about the job of locating and buying presents for friends and family. Mostly, winter was a cold and miserable time, with regular frost accompanied by thick snow. The frost often lasted for weeks through day and night, making things difficult at times and bursting many pipes as it penetrated deeper underground. There was no salt used on the roads in those days, and the paths and roads became treacherous to use safely, especially for the old people. Car drivers, and there were very few, had to fit chains on the driving wheels to enable them to move at all on the main roads, and with no chance of travelling on the minor ones.

I remember seeing a car pulling a sledge along London Road one day when there was very little or no other traffic on the road. The snow would be packed hard on the road after a

The medieval Newark Market Place, still at the commercial heart of the town.

few days, with the sun melting the surface in the daytime and the frost doing its worst at night to make it into a glass finish more suitable for skating than driving. If you were travelling alongside the Great North Road in the winter there was always a great deal of flood water in the fields near the roadside. Here the land had been scooped out to direct any water through the arches supporting the road, and thus preventing it from being washed away or flooded.

This water was frozen in the winter, making a fine area for skating which was used by many of the townspeople, who would turn out to take advantage of it. This was one of winter's pleasures that was available to everyone, young or old, free of charge.

As boys, a friend and I would start about two weeks before Christmas to cover an area alongside the London Road where

the better-off folk lived. We would go from one house to another singing Christmas carols – not just one carol and then go away, but several into which a great deal of feeling was put. We enjoyed the singing, and on many occasions we were invited into the house where we would sing as required by the owner. The family would often join in, making it a pleasant evening for them and us.

Singing was not an effort for either of us; we had both been auditioned by Tid Pratt for his choir and my friend did succeed, which meant going to church on Sundays. This was something I did not relish, with all the other options available. On occasions we were also given wine and presents, often being asked to visit again when a party was to take place. Not only was this a very enjoyable time for us, but we realized we were giving a great deal of pleasure to these people through our efforts. The rewards were usually great for us, also. The money we collected bought many of the presents for my family, as well as making me feel like a millionaire, with money in my pocket.

At Christmas time all the shops around the town centre joined in with some form of decoration, but it was the poultry shops that attracted my eye. All the birds would be hanging outside, still in full feather and with little cups under their beaks to catch the drops of blood from the killing. There were all types of birds hanging there above the pavement on the metal bars that were set up outside the shop for the purpose.

There was always a great deal of holly and mistletoe in evidence, carols were playing, and everyone seemed to be wrapped in the spirit of Christmas. All were being carried along at this wonderful time.

Bring Four of your Thieves

The Nottingham-born entertainer Leslie Crowther, now living in retirement near Bath after a horrific motorway accident that all but claimed his life, was always a great lover of pantomime – and of the showbiz lore that surrounded it.

One of his favourite stories concerned a low-budget production of *Ali Baba and his Forty Thieves*, the kind of show in which the effect of two-score thieves trooping into their cave was achieved by the same handful of actors exiting stage right, dashing around the back of the scenery, grabbing a different hat or scarf and re-entering stage left.

That was all very well, but what to do when the plot demanded that they should all be on the stage at the same time? 'That was easy,' Leslie recalled. 'Who can forget the immortal command: 'Come out of your cave, Ali Baba – and bring four of your thieves with you'?'

There was certainly no skimping in the old days at Nottingham's great panto theatre, the Theatre Royal. Its Forty Thieves show of 1885 so enthused the theatre's managing director, Tom Charles, that he was prompted 'to introduce into the Golden Armour of the Robber Band the beautiful ELECTRIC LIGHT. The expense of this Armour, and the Dresses, with Batteries and Appliances, has exceeded £1,000 . . .'

Come 1897 – when the travelling shows at the city's big October Goose Fair were already dabbling in early cinema –

Nottingham-born Leslie Crowther, a performer with panto close to his heart.

something altogether more ambitious than light bulbs was called for in that year's production of *Cinderella*. As a consequence, the concluding scene was Tableaux De Marbre, 'the Greatest Novelty of the Age, and never before presented in Great Britain'. It involved a troupe of thirty in elaborate costumes and wigs, with 'marvellous lighting effects entirely new for this theatre'; in three acts, the final one was ominously entitled *Le Massacre*. No wonder the best seats in the house set you back three shillings (15p). In the gods you got away with sixpence (2½p).

Cinders in 1897 was played by Lily Morris, in her later career a tough old duck noted for her eccentric dancing and

THEATRE ROYAL,

NOTTINGHAM.

Managing Director - - Mr. Thos. W. Charles.

Monday, Feb. 16th, & following Evenings,

SECOND EDITION

OF THE **GRAND PANTOMIME,** ENTITLED, THE

FORTY THIEVES!

NEW SONGS, NEW DANCES,

NEW DRESSES, & NEW BUSINESS.

The peculiar adaptability of the Story of the "FORTY THIEVES" for the introduction of Gorgeous Surroundings has induced Mr. CHARLES to introduce into the Golden Armour of the Robber Band the beautiful ELECTRIC LIGHT. The expense of this Armour, and the Dresses, with Batteries and Appliances, has exceeded **£1,000,** and Mr. CHARLES is indebted to G. E. SMITH, Esq., of Nottingham, for the interest he has taken in superintending the New Electric Room just added to the Theatre.

The Libretto written by Mr. F. R. GOODYER. Scenery of the most elaborate character has been Specially Painted by HARRY POTTS, JULES CAMUS, and K. J. McLENNAN. The Stage Management will be in the hands of Mr. HARRY FISCHER. The Overture and Incidental Music Composed, Selected, and Arranged by Mr. ALFRED R. WATSON. The Songs selected from the publications of Messrs. W. J. WILLCOCKS & CO., FRANCIS BROS. & DAY, LYON & HALL, HOPWOOD & CREW, CRAMER & CO., ORSBORNE & TUCKWOOD, J. BATH, C. SHEARD, F. AMOS & CO., and the Songs of Mr. MACDERMOTT sung by his permission. The Ballets and Incidental Dances arranged by Miss KATE PARADISE. The Harlequinade and Comic Scenes Invented by the Celebrated Clown, Mr. WATTIE HILDYARD. The Masks and Wigs by CLARKSON, London. Gorgeous Costumes have been executed by Mrs. MAY, London; Miss JESSON, Nottingham; and Mons. and Madam ALIAS, London. The Mechanical Changes of Scene by Mr. SEYMOUR. The Elaborate Properties and Paraphernalia by Mr. JONES. The Gas Arrangements by Mr. W. ADAMS. Limelight Arrangements by Mr. H. W. MARRIOTT. Electric Batteries and Steam Appliances under the Superintendence of Mr. WILLOUGHBY; and the Golden Electric Armour supplied by Mons. GENTY, London and Paris. The Silver Armour by KENNEDY & CO., Birmingham. The Jewellery and Ornaments by WHITE, London. The Costly Satins, Brocades, Flowers, and Trimmings by BURNETT & CO., London; DICKINSON and FAZAKERLEY, and R. PINDER, Nottingham. The whole Invented and Placed on the Stage under the Personal Superintendence of **THOS. W. CHARLES.**

THEATRE ROYAL
NOTTINGHAM.
Manager Mr. Thos. W. Charles.

SATURDAY, FEBRUARY 2nd, 1884
And EVERY EVENING until further Notice.

MORNING PERFORMANCE every Saturday, at Half-past Two.

SECOND EDITION
OF THE
GRAND PANTOMIME,
ENTITLED—

LITTLE BO-PEEP

INVENTED & PRODUCED BY THOS. W. CHARLES.
The Libretto written by F. R. GOODYER.

The Stage Management will be in the hands of Mr. Sidney Hayes, assisted by Mr. A. T. Macinnes. The Scenery will be of the most elaborate character from the brushes of Mr. Harry Potts, Mr. A. H. Groom, Mr. Charles Bellair, Mons. Jules Camus, & Mr. J. K. M'Lennan. The Overture and Incidental Music composed, selected, and arranged by Mr. Alfred R. Watson. The Ballets, Processions, and Incidental Movements arranged by that charming and accomplished Artiste, Miss Ange Russell. The Harlequinade and Comic Scenes invented by the Celebrated Clown, Mr. George R. Budd. The Gorgeous Costumes have been executed by Miss Jesson, of Nottingham. The exquisite Fairy Dresses suggested and made after Paintings given in the kindest manner, by Miss Florence St. John. The Mechanical Changes of Scene by Mr. Seymour. The Elaborate Properties and Paraphernalia by Mr. Jones. The Gas Arrangements by Mr. W. Adams. The Lime Light by W. Marriott. The whole invented and placed upon the Stage under the Personal Superintendence of THOS. W. CHARLES.

Opposite and above: no expense spared bills for pantomimes at Nottingham Theatre Royal in the 1880s. By the 1890s the timing had switched from February to Christmas.

the famous old music hall song 'Why Am I Always the Bridesmaid?' At this stage of her life, however, she could more than carry it off as a sweet and innocent beauty. The *Evening Post's* report, thousands of words long, tells us all we need to know about the show, which also featured the Darnley Brothers, Albert and Herbert, as the ugly sisters Saccharina and Dulcetina, Clara Bernard as Prince Peerless, the Tiller Troupe and Staveley's Merry Maids.

'There enters Miss Julia Kent as Popinjay, the Prince's valet, in a natty tiger dress,' the *Post* records. 'She sings *Dear Boy, Ta-ta* admirably. The call of the hunting horn heralds the appearance of the Prince, who introduces himself with a

Robin Hood as you have never seen him before – portrayed by Lily Langtry, an actress best remembered for her close relationship with Edward VII.

Not quite top of the bill: the Olympia Serenaders of Trent Bridge, 1911.

rollicking hunting song. The burden of the refrain is taken up lustily by the stage crowd, and the effect is very inspiring. The Prince returns thanks for the loyalty of the reception accorded to him, whereupon Quilmo reminds his august master that love for a sporting prince:

> . . . ne'er fails,
> Bearing in mind our own dear Edward Wales . . .

An apt remark which was keenly relished.

A disquisition upon various types of girls naturally paves the way for a complimentary allusion to the Nottingham maidens who are, we seem to have heard before, famed in unwritten history for their winsome looks.'

All this life, this vigour, this colour, was a hundred years ago. Yet clearly, the essence of pantomime has not changed vastly over a century. And when one considers the energy expended by the thigh-slapping Prince, the high-kicking Tiller girls, the warbling Miss Morris, no wonder the susceptible say that nowhere is the spirit of those who have gone before more apparent than on the stage of one of our great old theatres.

Garth Hepplewhite's Come-uppance

AMBROSE GADD

Ambrose Gadd wrote a monthly column, The Diary of a Stroller, in the old society magazine The Nottingham Observer. *It was strictly to be taken with a pinch of salt – residents of Beeston in December 1957, for instance, when this piece was published, will rack their brains in vain if they try to recall the likes of Aloysius Broom and Horace Dinwiddie – but it was an engaging column, and a welcome counterpoint to the* Observer's *staple diet of hunt ball pictures and starchy articles by the lesser nobility.*

It was shortly after eight o'clock on a bitter night that an assembly of thirty-odd Christmas carol singers huddled at a street corner in Beeston and prepared for the evening's stint.

I wondered why I was among them instead of sitting cosily behind one of the warm, well-lighted windows which spangled the surrounding gloom. But what could I do when a presentable young woman coyly straightened my tie, fluttered her eyelashes in an appealing way and asked me to join the carol group 'because they were short of men's voices'?

The conductor, Mr Aloysius Broom, controlled his singers not with a baton but with a rod of iron. He frowned at my first false note; he glared at the second. At the third he fixed me with a baleful eye, quite out of keeping with the Spirit of Goodwill, and announced in grating tones: 'I really think, Mr Gadd, you would assist us more by holding one of the lanterns.'

'Oh,' I said, taken aback. 'Do I really have to?'

'Either that,' he said firmly, 'or go round with the collecting box.'

I chose the lantern. The Spirit of Goodwill had suffered a body blow. 'And,' added Mr Broom fiercely, 'the next person who sings a wrong note can help you. I don't care who it is – and you'll learn I'm a man of my word.'

To complete my mortification, I saw just then that Master Horace Dinwiddie was also a member of the party. He was doubling himself up with evil glee. Those who remember the discomfiture I have suffered at the hands of this youthful Machiavelli, now rising twelve years of age, will understand my embarrassment.

I edged closer and actually had my hand poised to fetch him a well-merited clip of the ear when astonishment halted it in mid-swipe. He was actually clean – his hair neatly combed, his face shining with soap, his shoes gleaming.

'What are you doing here?' I demanded, hoarsely.

'Keep off!' squawked Horace. 'I'm singing the treble solo. I'll tell Mr Broom . . .'

Thunder clouds gathered on the conductor's brow. I lowered my hand. 'No horseplay, please!' he said. 'We are here to sing carols, not enjoy ourselves. Besides, Mr Hepplewhite will arrive any minute . . .'

Some female let out a pleased squeal. 'Garth Hepplewhite? Actually singing with us? Oh!'

Mr Broom smiled smugly. 'Yes, indeed, ladies!' More squeals. He might well have been announcing the impending arrival of Mr Frankie Vaughan or Mr Elvis Presley. Even the boy Horace contributed an awed 'Coo!'

Garth Hepplewhite, alighting just then from a taxi, proved to be a portly, rather pompous looking man of shortish stature. His appearance did nothing to restore the Spirit of Goodwill so far as I was concerned, but the feminine portion of the contingent remained atwitter until Mr Broom rapped the music stand.

'We shall continue with *Good King Wenceslas*,' he announced. 'Come, Horace . . .'

'Eh? Eh? What's this?' asked Hepplewhite sharply. 'Who's this boy?'

Mr Broom said 'Oh, er, he's the page . . .'

You get the idea, I hope. After specified choral work, Horace's treble was due to pipe up with:

> Sire, the night is darker now
> And the wind blows colder . . .

Then Good King Wenceslas, alias Hepplewhite, would boom out:

> Mark my footsteps, good my page,
> Tread thou in them boldly . . .

'Nonsense!' snorted Hepplewhite. 'Old fashioned and quite unnecessary. We'll just have the choir – and my solo part, of course. Go away, boy!'

I was standing quite near at the time. Obviously, the man hadn't the slightest idea he was meddling with dynamite.

'Look,' I said to him, in a low voice. 'I wouldn't press the point, if I were you . . .'

He gave me a very nasty look. 'When I require advice,' he said loftily, 'I will ask for it . . .'

The Spirit of Goodwill took one hurried glance and disappeared round the corner. Horace, meantime, was muttering to himself in a markedly peeved manner and scuffing the toes of his shoes.

'Don't I sing my piece, then?' he demanded.

'You do not,' said Mr Broom. 'Make yourself useful by handing out the music and taking round the collecting box. Carol No. 1 on our list . . .'

Master Dinwiddie obeyed with ill grace.

I clutched the lantern pole throughout *Good King Wenceslas* and *Hark, the Herald Angels*. The choir didn't do so badly, I thought. There were no spontaneous bursts of applause from the public, but at least no one emptied jugs from upper windows.

'No. 3,' announced Mr Broom. 'Then we will move on.'

Horace handed round the copies. Mr Broom raised his baton.

Something went sadly askew with the harmony. While the choir embarked softly on the smooth sibilance of *Silent Night*, Garth Hepplewhite's powerful tones boomed out simultaneously in a different key with *God Rest Ye Merry, Gentlemen*. The appalling discord lasted for about three bars, then trailed away into consternation.

A startled passer-by said loudly that we ought to be ashamed of ourselves. Somewhere a baby began to cry.

Spot the dreadful Garth Hepplewhite.

Horace had given our star singer the wrong piece of music.

I went across and thrust the lantern pole into Garth Hepplewhite's nerveless fingers. At the same time, Horace handed him the collecting box.

Then the two of us slipped away into the friendly Christmas darkness in pursuit of the Spirit of Goodwill, without waiting to see whether Mr Broom really was a man of his word.

from

It's Trew Worram Tellin' Yer

ANNE SPENCER

The book of this splendid title was published by Sutton-in-Ashfield Living Memory Group in 1987, drawing on the childhood recollections of the town's older residents. This piece by Anne Spencer recalls the 1920s – one big difference between then and now being that Christmas seventy years ago did not begin in October. In other ways, for the young child, not a lot seems to have changed. The excitement spans the decades . . .

Christmas always brings a lump to my throat. It was the excitement of what I should give and what I should get, and I always think of my childhood at Christmas. It started about a week before. The copper would be stoked up and Mam would make the Christmas puddings and boil them in their basin, clean rag on the top. The smell was delicious!

Dad would start making two rugs with cloth remnants from the factory. Mam would cut up the beautiful coloured pieces into strips. The reason Dad made the two rugs was to put one down on Christmas morning and to raffle one to make us a good Christmas. Dad was in the building trade and he couldn't work from November to March; we only had

£1.50 dole money, nothing else, and 10*s* 2*d* or 51p of that was for the rent.

So much for that; let's get back to the excitement of Christmas. Come two days before Christmas, Mam would dye the curtains a beautiful colour, and then the day before the big day Mam would put the copper on to boil the ham another time. We didn't mind the mess the copper made. Christmas Eve we used to go carol singing, and would get about a shilling. My Dad used to say: 'Go and buy your Mam a present.' My sister and brothers and I would rush to the shops and look at the presents in the windows. I bet we'd be looking at least half an hour at all the gifts, and then we'd all decide what to buy. It was either a milk jug or a teapot or a sugar basin. Then we'd hurry home and sing a carol to fetch Mam and Dad to the door and we'd all say: 'Here's a present for both of you!' Mam would be nearly in tears. After a hot drink I would go with Dad to finish the shopping, to the market stalls with their swinging gas lanterns. What a sight! Mam would be at home finishing the baking and looking after my brothers and sister.

Christmas Eve! What excitement! We would all hang our stockings at the bottom of our beds, and on Christmas morning, as soon as we were awake, we would shout: 'Has he been?' He always left our presents in Mam and Dad's bedroom, and they would shout back: 'He hasn't been yet, because the wine and mince pie are still on the top of the stairs.' After our shouts they would say: 'Have a look to see if the wine and mince pie have gone.' We couldn't get out of bed quick enough. What excitement when we found the wine and mince pie *had* gone. We'd dash into Mam and Dad's bedroom to see all the presents for us.

After playing with our toys in bed we would all go downstairs for breakfast. What a sight! Mam and Dad had trimmed the holly tree and hung up the decorations after we had gone to bed. The curtains and rug looked beautiful, and the

smell of pork roasting in the oven is one of my happiest memories. Then came dinner. There would be threepenny pieces for all of us in the Christmas pudding. After dinner we would go to Grandma's. She would give us all a small present and we would wish her and Aunty Ada a Merry Christmas. Then we would go home – and the sight that met our eyes! The table would be loaded with the boiled ham, Christmas cake, mince pies and lemon curds. What a feast! After tea we would go carol singing and we would get about threepence apiece. We would have supper and to bed we would go happy and contented.

On Boxing Day we would have breakfast and dinner with goodies that were left from Christmas Day, and after that we would go to the cinema with the threepence we had earned carol singing. The cinema was in the afternoon, and as everyone came out, the management would give us an apple and an orange to take home. Those are the Christmases as a child that I will never forget.

Robin Hood and his Little Friends

This seasonal 'Tale of the Merry Men of the Greenwood' was published in the Playbox *annual for very young children in 1924. It is not a work of literary genius, but is typical of the way in which the deeds of Robin Hood have been elaborated on*

in children's literature over the centuries. Note, too, the cod medieval language, forsooth. As for the two little children going off into the forest with the big stranger, and Maid Marian recruiting Brenda for the kitchen and Egbert to look after the horses, how politically incorrect was the medieval merry man – merry person – of seventy years ago.

'Isn't this lovely, Egbert?' whispered little Brenda as she looked round the big market place with shining eyes. It was Christmas Eve, and Nottingham Fair was in full swing. Nobody minded the deep snow on the ground, for everyone was happy, and even the Norman soldiers there were too busy to notice the little Saxons as they wandered along by the booths and stalls.

'Even if we have no money, we can have a Christmas feast by looking, can't we, Brenda?' said her brother. And with open eyes they stared at the tumblers and mountebanks, the fat geese and fatter pigs, the minstrels and ballad singers. Then they stopped in front of one of the stalls, heaped high with gingerbread in all shapes and sizes.

'If only I had money, Brenda,' said the little boy, 'I would buy you a big gingerbread doll.'

'And that fine horse for yourself, Egbert!' The little girl's blue eyes grew bright at the thought of such a feast.

'What d'ye lack? What d'ye lack?' cried the cross looking baker from behind the stall, but they shook their heads.

'We have no money,' said Egbert.

'Then haste away and ask your father for some,' replied the baker. 'Tell him this gingerbread is good enough for King John himself!'

At the mention of her father the little girl began to cry, and her brother put his arm around her. 'We have no father or mother, fair sir,' he said, 'and we were only looking at your brave show.' Comforting his little sister, he moved away, but a

stout dame passing by saw the girl's tears. She had a live goose under one arm and a heap of evergreen under the other, but she fumbled in her purse and pushed a silver penny into Brenda's hand.

''Tis Yule Feast, child,' she said. 'Don't cry, but buy thyself some gingerbread!' Before the children could thank her, she had bustled by, but the baker had seen her give the children the money, and his greedy eyes glistened as they came back to the stall.

'Give me thy money!' he demanded, and Egbert handed him the silver penny.

'We would have a gingerbread doll and a horse, please,' he said, but the stallholder shook his head.

'You will not have anything at all. Go away, you are beggar children!' he cried.

'But – but you have taken our money,' said Egbert. 'And we have had no gingerbread. It was for our Christmas feast!'

'Go away, I tell you,' repeated the baker, 'or I will give you to the Normans!'

Running round from the back of his stall, he caught hold of Egbert and his sister and pushed them away. Too frightened of the Normans to say much, the little Saxons were moving away when Egbert turned round and cried stoutly:

'You are a thief, Master Baker! We did give you money!'

'Aye, that he did, for I saw him!' came in a big, deep voice from behind them – and Egbert, looking around, saw a big woodman staring fiercely at the baker.

'I know you of old, friend Wilfred,' said the woodman, 'and the boy is right: thou art a thief. Now give him his cakes, and right quickly, too, before I turn over thy stall!'

He looked so angry that the baker's face went pale, and he eagerly handed Egbert a gingerbread doll and horse.

'That is not good value,' said the woodman. 'Here, I will show you how to serve children. Hold out thy hands,' he said

Market Place, Nottingham under snow (above), and the Market, Retford (below), both seen early this century.

to Brenda, and as she did so he filled them to overflowing with gingerbread horses and dolls and carts and medals.

'Now go right merrily and feast well, sweetheart,' said the big woodman. 'And as for you,' he continued to the frightened baker, 'I only wish my friends in Lincoln green were here with me. 'Twould be a sorry figure you would cut, for all your friendship with the Normans.'

The baker was too afraid to say anything, but he only scowled as the woodman, with an arm around each of the children, led them through the fair to the edge of the wood.

'Now here you will be safe for your home,' he told them, 'and I must leave you.'

'We are grateful for your kindness, brave sir,' said Egbert.

'Tut! tut!' said their big friend. 'Some day you may be able to repay it. Thou art a brave lad.' And with a pat on the boy's shoulder and a kiss on Brenda's curly head, he went back to the fair.

Munching their gingerbread, the children slowly made their way to their lonely cottage. They were quite at home in the forest, but suddenly Egbert looked behind him and stopped. 'Look, Brenda, there is the baker coming – and yet there are Normans with him!'

'Perhaps he has come after us,' said Brenda. 'Oh, dear, let us hide.' Quick as a couple of rabbits the two little Saxons slipped into the undergrowth by the side of the road.

A minute later the baker came along. With him were half a dozen Norman soldiers, but he was not talking of Brenda and Egbert.

'I am certain it was Robin Hood, and he came this way with two children,' he said. They had all stopped, and were looking down the road.

'There is no sight of him now,' said one of the soldiers suspiciously.

'Then if he has not come along, he will very shortly,' said Wilfred. 'Wait a while and you will catch him.'

''Twill be ill for you if we don't,' replied the Norman. 'We have orders to go and meet the waggon that is to bring us our Christmas cheer, and have no time to spend on a wild goose chase.'

'Have no fear,' said the baker. 'I have seen Robin before, and know his ways right well. Even an hour since he robbed me of goods to give to two beggar children. He will come this way, true enough.'

'And there is a purse of gold for his capture. A right welcome gift for such as us,' added one of the other soldiers with a laugh. 'Come, I would handle that purse. We will rest and wait for Robin here.'

Suiting the action to the words, he began to hide himself in the bushes, followed by his companions. 'An excellent idea,' said Wilfred, 'and while you rest yourselves I will wander back and see if I can see aught of our friend.'

Hidden amongst the bracken, Brenda looked at her brother. 'That was Robin Hood who helped us,' she whispered.

'And the Normans are after him,' added Egbert. 'Come along; we must warn him.'

Without another word they crept as silently as possible through the bracken and undergrowth until, quite out of sight of either Wilfred or the Normans, they got back to the path. As fast as they could scamper they ran down the road, and they were nearly back to the town when they saw the figure of the woodman coming along. He was carrying a bag of food on his back and singing a Christmas carol as he walked.

'Hullo, children!' he cried. 'Are you going back for more gingerbread, then?'

'Please, are you Robin Hood?' asked Egbert, rather frightened. The big woodman stopped laughing, and grew serious.

'Why do you ask, my boy?' he said.

'Because if you are, there are Normans up the road with Wilfred the baker, and they are waiting to capture you,' said Egbert quickly.

'Here, what is this?' replied the woodman, and he looked from one to the other of the children, as if unable to believe his ears.

'There are Normans,' said Brenda, nodding her head. 'They are hiding in the bushes.'

'Well, I am Robin Hood,' said the big woodman, 'and you have been able to repay me sooner than you thought. Come with me now. We will soon settle the Normans!'

Without further words he left the road and dived into the bushes, followed by the children. For half a mile they walked. Then they entered a little clearing, and putting his fingers to his lips, Robin Hood gave a shrill whistle. Within a few moments there appeared from every direction archers clad in Lincoln green, all members of the great outlaw band.

'Ho, my merry men!' cried Robin. 'The Normans are along the road waiting for me with Wilfred the baker. They would have caught me well enough if it had not been for the two children here.'

A big man came forward and looked suspiciously at Brenda and her brother. 'Normans!' he said. 'There were no signs of Normans when I came along the road a little time since. These children tell the truth, Robin, think you?'

'Oh, aye, Little John,' said the outlaw chief, 'of that I am right certain.'

'If you please,' said little Brenda, 'the Normans have only just gone along the road. They were sent to meet the waggon bringing their Christmas cheer when they met Wilfred, who told them about Robin Hood.'

For a moment both Robin Hood and Little John were puzzled. Then they both burst out into a roar of laughter.

'Christmas cheer, eh? They have left it unprotected,' said Robin. 'Why, we could do with some of that, and I know half a dozen poor families who could do with the rest. It is better fitted to be eaten by Saxons than by Normans. What say you, my merry men?'

The shout of laughter that went up showed that his men shared their leader's thoughts. While they were busy getting ready a gentle-faced lady came up and laid her hand on Robin's arm. He turned to her with a smile.

'Greetings, Maid Marian!' he said. 'I am glad you have come. Here are two little friends of mine; they have just saved me from capture, and will spend the Christmas Feast with us. We are just off to get the good things which have been sent to the Normans – a little mistake we are going to correct.'

'I am pleased to see them, as well as you, Robin,' said Maid Marian. 'Come along, children; we have a long way to go yet to our cave where we spend our Christmas, but there are ponies for all of us.'

Both Egbert and his sister could ride as well as they could walk; all the children who lived in the forest could ride the shaggy little ponies, and they had no trouble in following Maid Marian right into the heart of the Forest. There they found some wonderful caves where the outlaws lived. They were nicely furnished, and much more comfortable than the broken-down cottage where the children lived.

'Come, we must get a meal ready now,' said Maid Marian. 'You help me with the pots, Brenda, while Egbert takes the ponies to their stables.' Both the children were soon so busy that they did not notice how the time went, when suddenly they heard the rumbling of wheels outside the cave, and then a great shout of welcome.

What a sight met their eyes when they ran out. There was a great Norman waggon loaded high with good things. Sides of bacon, sacks of flour, honey cakes, apples and pears, and

A chilly time of it for the forest ponies.

home-made wines. And on top of it all, looking very frightened, was Wilfred the baker. He was blindfolded, so that he should not know the way to Robin Hood's secret hiding place, for which the children were thankful, in case he should recognize them.

'He was looking for me, but I found him first,' said Robin Hood, pointing to the unhappy man. 'Now, my fine fellows,' he cried to his band, 'get busy unloading this waggon. The Normans are waiting for it, you know.'

It did not take them long to empty it, and then Robin Hood called his men together. By his side was Wilfred the baker.

'This man,' said Robin sternly, 'tried to sell me to the Normans. He failed, but I will not punish him; he can punish

Robin Hood and his men as seen by *Playbox*, 1924.

himself. Fill this waggon with snow, and let Wilfred the baker drive it back to the Normans, and tell them that Robin Hood has captured their Christmas cheer. That shall be his punishment. Hungry men are usually cross men . . .'

A shout of laughter went up from the outlaws, and the baker's face went paler than ever.

'Good Master Robin,' he cried to the outlaw chief, 'pray let me go! If I have to drive that waggon back filled with snow, the Normans will whip me full sore.'

'And serve you right!' said Little John. 'If you had had your way, our Robin would have spent Christmas in a Norman dungeon. Get you gone, and thank our good chief that you have suffered so lightly.'

And with shouts of laughter the outlaws piled the waggon high with snow. With a smack on the ponies' backs they drove them out on to the road, leaving the unkind baker to get on as best he could. What the Normans did say to Wilfred, the children never found out. For after the most glorious Christmas feast they had ever had, Maid Marian said that she could not spare Brenda, as she was useful in the cave, while Egbert could do anything with the ponies. It meant that they never went back to their old home, but stayed with the outlaws, where they had many more adventures.

Riot at the Soup House

ABIGAIL GAWTHERN

*Abigail Gawthern was a dedicated chronicler of Nottingham life in the late eighteenth and early nineteenth centuries, and there was much interest in her diaries when Adrian Henstock edited them and had them published by the Thoroton Society of historians in 1980. The Christmas Day bread riot of 1800 came as the climax of a year of desperate unrest, hunger and disease, as the war with France raged. In the first half of the year, the price of a quartern loaf was anything from 15*d *to 18*d, *while wheat was fetching as much as 145 shillings a quarter. A riot in Nottingham on 19 April saw food stalls robbed, and the military sent in to quell the crowds. An uprising from the last day of August to 3 September was broken up only by torrential storms – and then came Christmas, a time of year notoriously hostile to the underprivileged. As can be seen, Abigail Gawthern was not of that number.*

12 December 1800

Mr Ray's ball. He sent us tickets, we went, stayed till 2 o'clock; a crowded room.

18 December

Miss Charlotte Mettam married Mr Longden; they and Miss

Mettam set off for London directly after the ceremony; they were married at St Mary's by Mr George Mettam, and Dr Haines gave the bride away.

19 December

The Prince of Wales came through this town to go to Lord Moira's at Castle Donington; a Swiss servant went before the carriage smoking a pipe; the Prince sent for horses from the Black's Head to the Trent Bridge to avoid stopping in the town.

25 December

Christmas Day. Mrs Frost, Mrs Brough, Miss Moises, Mr Neville, Mr Partridge and Mr Basil Marriott spent the day here; some rioting this evening at the soup house; they broke

To the Inhabitants of the Town of

NOTTINGHAM.

THE MAGISTRATES are very much concerned to obſerve the continuance of riot and depredation in this town: they therefore REPEAT their commands to all perſons *immediately to diſperſe to their ſeveral habitations*: And all maſters of families are ſtrictly charged to keep at home their reſpective apprentices and ſervants ——Should *this* Caution remain unattended to, and the peace of the town *not* be reſtored, the *moſt coercive and ſevere meaſures* will

IMMEDIATELY BE PURSUED

to enforce the preſervation of the public peace.

THE MAGISTRATES earneſtly entreat their Fellow-Townſmen to bear it impreſſed upon their minds, That the TOWN is dependent upon the COUNTRY for its ſupply of Bread corn—that unleſs peace and good order be reſtored, it is impoſſible for any exertions to induce the Farmers to ſend their corn to the town; and, conſequently, thoſe who diſturb the public peace are the perſons who *really* and *truly* prevent the poſſibility of the friends of public tranquility from alleviating the ſufferings which they ſincerely deplore.

Exertions have been made, and are making, by the Magiſtrates, to BRING DOWN THE PRICE OF CORN—but without *internal* peace it will be impoſſible for that ſupply to enter the town which can alone produce a

REDUCTION OF THE PRICE

of Corn and Flour.

BY ORDER,

Geo. Coldham, *Town Clerk.*

Nottingham, 2d September, 1800.

(Burbage and Stretton, Printers, &c. Nottingham.)

Fig. 4 *Broadsheet regarding bread riots in Nottingham, 1800*

'The moft fevere meafures . . .' The town clerk's proclamation at the height of the Nottingham bread riots of 1800.

the windows. The Blues were out all night; the mob attempted to set fire to Mr Chamberlain's stacks at Lenton, but soldiers prevented them.

29 December
A vast deal of snow. A large mob went on the Forest; a troop of the 17th Light Dragoons came in this morning between three and four o'clock. They left Birmingham yesterday. They were attending divine service, and were ordered out of church before the service was finished.

Poor Owd 'Oss

PAT MAYFIELD

Pat Mayfield's Legends of Nottinghamshire, *published in 1976, included this version of the once widespread* Poor Owd 'Oss *mumming play. The guising tradition lived on in Mansfield, to the north of the county, long after it had petered out in most other communities.*

This is a very old play which used to be performed in the Mansfield area around Christmas time. I am greatly indebted to Mr Mellors of Mansfield, whose research several years ago uncovered it, and for his permission for me to reproduce it here. Mansfield was always a small town, and this play we

Mansfield Market, where so many Christmas presents were bought when money was scarce.

must presume was an elementary form of pantomime. The men would perform in public houses as well as in the houses of the gentry. The custom was still alive in the 1860s but since then has faded away altogether until now it is impossible even to obtain a copy of the words.

Entitled *Poor Owd 'Oss*, it is of course partly in dialect, but to alter it into basic English would I feel be wrong and would in fact spoil the play. The 'owd 'oss' was performed by a man who was draped in a dark cloth. The horse's head was probably fashioned out of papier-mâché and was fixed to a stick. Here are the words of the play:

By your leave gentlemen all
Your pardon I do crave,
Excusing me for being so bold
To see what sport we'll have.

There's more in the company now,
They're following on behind,
They've sent us on before,
Admission for to find.

These lads they are but young,
Ne'er acted here before,
They'll do the best they can
And the best can do no more.

The horse is now brought in for the first time:

Co-oop Co-oop Co-oop.
This is my poor owd 'oss
That's carried me many a mile,
Over hedges, over ditches, over high barred gates and stiles.

This Poor Owd 'Oss looks even more ill-fed than usual.

But now he's growing owder.
And his nature doth decay,
He's forced to snap the shortest grass
That grows upon the 'ighway.
Poor owd 'oss.

Now when this 'oss was young sir,
And in his youth and prime,
His master rode upon him
And thought him something fine.
His pretty little shoulders,
They were so plump and round,
But now they're decayed and rotten,
I'm afraid he is not sound.
Poor owd 'oss.

His feed was once the best of corn and hay,
That ever grew in cornfields,
Or in a meadow lay.
He's eaten all my hay sir,
He's spoil-ed all my straw,
He's neither fit to ride upon
Nor in the team to draw.
Poor owd 'oss.

His hide unto a tanner
I will so freely give,
His body to the hounds sir,
I'd rather 'im die than live,
Then hang him, whip him, stick him,
A hunting we will go,
He's neither fit to ride upon,
He is no use at all.
Poor owd 'oss.

The blacksmith was now called for, and he had to make attempts to shoe the horse. Consequently a lot of rough play then took place among all the members of the cast, saying as they did so:

> Now for us to shoe this 'oss, sir,
> He is no use at all sir,
> He would soon a' worried the blacksmith
> And his box o' nails an' all.
> Poor owd 'oss.

After the fun was over drinks were called for the players and a question put to the horse: 'Could the 'oss manage a drink?' Needless to say he could. The horse's head was, however, not removed while he took his drink. The jaws were so arranged that a mug or tankard could be placed inside them so that the 'oss got his refreshments – to the amusement of all the spectators.

The Pilgrims' First Christmas

ROLAND G. USHER

The now almost lost village of Scrooby, in the north of the county between Retford and Bawtry, was the home of several of the Pilgrim Fathers who sailed to America to escape real or feared religious persecution at the hands of the Stuarts in 1620. Brewster, Smythe, Clifton, Bradford, Robinson, Sandys . . . figures at the heart of the Pilgrim movement were Scrooby men, and their visiting American descendants are still to be met occasionally wandering the now largely green fields of their forefathers' home. The Mayflower *sailed from England in August 1620 – from Southampton, and not from Plymouth, as is so often supposed. The place the Pilgrims chose as their first settlement was already mapped as Plymouth before they arrived there. This account of their first Christmas on alien soil is from Roland G. Usher's* The Pilgrims and their History, *published in New York in 1918.*

The first stage of the great enterprise successfully accomplished, the difficulties in their path one after another surmounted, a greater problem now loomed before them – how could the transition from ship to shore be safely made and the colony established on the soil of the New World? Monday, 18 December found the Pilgrims early ashore. That

day and the two succeeding were consumed in eager and thorough explorations of the harbour, the rivers, the forests and the soil. On the twentieth a vote was taken and the majority elected to build the new settlement on what Bradford called the first site, evidently that selected by the leaders who came in the shallop a week or more previously. The name Plymouth they found on Smith's map of New England, and retained it.

The site was well adapted for a permanent fishing and trading factory. Though the *Mayflower* was compelled to lie in the outer harbour on account of the shallow water at low tide, the harbour was deep enough for a ship of no more than eighty tons to anchor near the shore. The second fact which impressed them was the number of fish they saw and the larger amount they conjectured would be present in the

A reconstruction of the *Mayflower* at Jamestown, Virginia.

proper season. Whales they had seen off Provincetown; they had been told by the crew of the vast profit from the sale of the oil, and they judged in the sublimity of their ignorance that it would be easy to kill one. Seals also they saw and deemed valuable. Thus two prime requisites were answered. The amount of cleared land on either side of what came to be called the Town Brook also attracted them to the site. A good many acres of cornfields of the Patuxets, dead from the plague of three years before, were unused, and after testing the soil, they concluded it to be rich and sufficiently deep.

The small rivers and brooks emptying into the harbour provided an abundance of water, while at a distance of an eighth of a mile stood abundant timber for their houses and for the cut lumber, which they expected to export to England, where wood was scarce and expensive. Furthermore, the site was protected by nature, for on the east the harbour and on the south, the Town Brook, in a little ravine, prevented attack by the Indians. On the west an abrupt hill a hundred and sixty-five feet high gave them a location for their cannon, commanding the only easy approaches to the new town from the open fields to the north.

After two days of storm and rain, they set to work on 23 December, and for three days cut timber with great diligence. The difficulties of their task were considerable, for their headquarters, the *Mayflower*, was one-and-a-half miles from shore, and they must row back and forth constantly. They were compelled to carry out the timber itself an eighth of a mile from the woods without draught animals to assist. There were in all only forty-four adult men, many of whom were by this time ill. The first Christmas, therefore, was spent in hard work – for like most Protestant bodies of the time, the Pilgrims declined to celebrate the day, because they could find no warrant for it in the Scriptures. Two more days of rain interfered with the work, but on the twenty-eighth they laid

out the town along the brook, and assigned locations for a 'common house' to be used as an assembly hall, and for several dwelling houses. After more rain and cold during the first week in January, the work went on at a more rapid rate and without intermission. Jones and his men went out in the shallop, and after some ado caught three seals and one codfish. Apparently an expedition whose prime object was the catching of fish had arrived with no practical knowledge of the sort of fishing which New England afforded. On 7 January, to facilitate the work, the company was divided into nineteen 'families', thus putting the boys and servants under the supervision of the older married men.

Signs of Trouble

ALBERT WALKER

Former PC Albert Walker has written two books of recollections of his life as a policeman in the north of the county, Walking the Beat with Albert RN. *This piece, from the second book, published in 1990, recalls a hard learning process in the village of Collingham.*

It was on 2 July, 1957 that my wife Cath, with Gladys, Robert, Christine and John arrived at Collingham – along with me, of course – where I had taken over residence as the

new village constable. From then up to the first Christmas, I spent the time learning the beat, which comprised the villages of South Collingham, Langford, Holme, Danethorpe and Brough on the south side, with North Collingham, Besthorpe and South Scarle on the north side. In those days, Collingham was split into two separate parishes.

As I moved around on my pedal cycle I became ever more grateful at having landed such a plum picking of a station, surrounded by beautiful countryside.

Soon, Christmas was upon us with the infectious spirit it brings, and feeling full of goodwill I thought I would put up a poster on the police notice board to our parishioners. I set to with a large poster-size sheet of paper, and I remember printing on it in big, bold capitals something like: PC WALKER and Mrs WALKER wish everybody in this and the surrounding villages a Very Merry Xmas and a Happy and Prosperous New Year. I decorated the poster up with drawings of holly, mistletoe and Christmas trees, and we reckoned it looked lovely. A week before Christmas I pinned it to the notice board in the front garden of the police house. I think there was a Stolen Property poster on the board at the time as well.

That same day – it was mid afternoon, and just a couple of hours after putting up the poster – I was in the back kitchen having a cup of tea with the wife when we became aware of someone banging loudly on the office door, followed by the incessant ringing of the doorbell. I thought 'here's trouble' as I dived through the office door. Taking the catch off, I yanked the front door open and there stood the Sergeant, somewhat red-faced.

'Hello, Sarge. Trouble?' said I.

'Trouble?' said he. 'Who's stuck that Christmas poster up out there on that police notice board?'

Astounded, I said: 'Me, Sarge. Why?'

There stood the sergeant, somewhat red-faced.

'Why?' said he. 'You mean to say why?' And here he paused for a breather before going on: 'Look lad, you don't do things like that. It's just not done, so get it down. That board is an official one, to let folks know who's been murdered or about robberies and missing property and missing-from-homers. It's not for wishing everybody a Merry Christmas.'

With that he stomped off, jumped into the little Ford Anglia section car and shot off along the road still muttering to himself. Dejectedly, I took the poster down. I thought: 'Where's his Christmas spirit?'

The following Springtime, I'd grown my first lot of lettuce, cauliflower and cabbage plants to put out in the back garden. There were far too many for me, and so once more the practising Christian took over. I did the plants up into 'scores' and rolled them up in newspaper, each little packet held together with an elastic band. I then popped the lot into a

metal bucket and placed them on a small table outside the gates leading into the police house with a card – another card. In bold writing it said: HELP YOURSELVES – FREE. This I pinned on to the front edge of the table, and went in. At the end of what had been a beautiful day, I went outside to fetch the table and bucket in. I found they had helped themselves, all right. They'd even nicked my bucket. I thought to myself, perhaps that's why the Sergeant didn't want me to wish everybody a Merry Christmas.

Christmas at the Workhouse

ONE WHO HAS SEEN BETTER DAYS

If the Victorian scandal sheet The Owl *did nothing else of lasting worth, it left us this astonishing documentary evidence of life in Nottingham's York Street workhouse in the 1880s. Published in the Christmas Day number of 1886, it is remarkable for painting the picture from the point of view of an inmate, rather than of the board officials or of well-meaning visitors who, as the writer reflects, saw an extremely rosy version of events on their Christmas Day visits. Of course the account is partial – the magazine was proudly anti-establishment and iconoclastic – but it nevertheless rings true.*

Interestingly, it is almost exactly contemporary with George R. Sims's Christmas Day in the Workhouse, *a ballad which, for all its openness to parody, was a savage indictment of the Poor Law of 1834. Obviously, liberal thinking of the 1880s was swinging violently against the system – yet it was not until 1929, in the lifetime of our present Queen, that it was erased from the statute book.*

It is necessary that the reader should be carried on 'fancy's wings' through the portals and into the precincts of the workhouse before he can fully realize the picture of its interior life. I write from actual experience, and may be able to take the perusers of this article, in thought, with me. As one of the unfortunate individuals whom the great depression of trade has driven for shelter within the grim enclosure situated in York Street, Nottingham, I will attempt to give the reader a truthful and graphic description. Let me confine myself to an outline of facts. Reduced to the greatest straits, and desirous of keeping in the path of rectitude, I was compelled to seek relief at the hands of our indulgent ratepayers, and accordingly turned my steps towards York Street. Entering the waiting room adjoining the relieving officers' sanctums, I found myself surrounded by a group of women wanting to receive in turn their weekly outdoor dole. I stood some time expecting a call from one of the occupants of the sacred office, but to my surprise found myself forestalled by an able-bodied man who had come on the same quest.

Presently my ears were offended by uncouth language issuing apparently from one of the said sanctums. 'Well, what do you want?' queried an individual from behind the partition, with all the pomposity of a parish beadle.

'I want an order for admission to the house, as I am quite destitute.'

NOTTINGHAM GORDON MEMORIAL HOME

FOR DESTITUTE WORKING BOYS.

Founded at a Public Meeting held at the Exchange Hall, on June 10, 1885, and formally opened by the Right Hon. Lord Belper, on December 18, 1885.

The Gordon Memorial Home for destitute boys, opened in the week before Christmas in 1885.

'Destitute? A strong, able man like you, destitute? Why, I should be ashamed of myself to come and sponge on the ratepayers if I were like you' – forgetting that he is one of the greatest sponges on the ratepayers.

After further bullying and browbeating the unfortunate applicant was asked: 'Where did you sleep last night?' The

reply not being satisfactory to the bumptious officer, that personage said: 'Well, you'll have to go into the tramp ward before you can get an order here.'

On hearing this I slipped out of the office, strolled pensively round the Forest, then unconsciously headed Carrington way, wondering all the time why it seemed imperative that a man should have a course of 'crummy' in the Tramp Ward before he was considered a fit candidate for admission into the body of the house. There was no alternative for me but to seek the Tramp Ward at night, and I passed through all the miseries which were so graphically described by some kindred spirit in *The Owl* a few weeks since. Next morning but one, I presented myself before the officer of my district. He was apparently in a jovial humour, as he was humming the favourite air *You'll Remember Me*, while the officer in the adjoining department glanced towards me with a scowl as black as night through his official goggles. My appearance at the pigeon hole somewhat altered the tone of the singing man. Even a good fellow like him has to assume the regulation frown on such occasions, while the massive carbuncle ring he wore reminded me painfully that I too had once been coxcomb enough to bedizen my fingers. He condescended to ask my business, I explained my case and the usual verbosity followed. Not wishing to bandy words, I had qualified myself by gathering a 'few friends' to take in with me, so the admission order was granted, and I was permitted to enter the house. I was received the same night into the able-bodied 'day ward', a full-blown, fustian-clad pauper.

I was presented with a tin medal to be hung over my bed, on which was pasted a number corresponding to the one on my shirt, stockings, and neckerchief. How do you like my suit? A pair of trousers with no pockets, a vest ditto, a jacket with a solitary button and button-hole, and – no it ain't – yes it is – a miniature pocket, justly supposed to be a sufficiently

commodious receptacle to contain all the heterogeneous mass of an indoor pauper's property. A piece of rag for a pocket handerchief, as he is not supplied with that necessary article, a comb, a piece of soap, pipe and tobacco, needles, thread, any scraps of food, are crammed indiscriminately into this apology for a pocket which adorns the pauper's jacket. No wonder that the ingenious contrive clandestine pouches in the linings of the vests, as even in a workhouse there are men who have feelings of common decency left, and do not care to have their food mixed with small tooth comb, carbolic soap and mucous wiper. The able-bodied ward, styled 'No. 2 Day Ward', is a room about eighteen or twenty feet by about ten feet. In this space are crammed about eighty men. The stifling atmosphere is something to remember. On my entrance I found that active preparations were being made for the annual festival. Coloured paper in profusion had been kindly given by Messrs Goater, Ford, and other local firms, whilst plenty of holly and other evergreens had been contributed by his Grace the Duke of St Albans, Colonel Seely, Mr Clifton, Captain Holden and other county gentlemen.

An old soldier – whose taste in decorative and other artistic work is deserving of a better sphere – was preparing the various devices for ornamenting the large dinner hall and other principal parts of the house. One of the assistant bakers was also busy in a similar manner, brightening the old men's ward. Several precepts and texts were arranged on the ward walls, one in particular being noticeable, the threadbare quotation: 'He that giveth to the poor, lendeth to the Lord'. For some reason, the worthy Boss of the House ordered another one to be substituted, which met with his approval. It was singularly suggestive, being worded: 'Come let us join our friends above'. I could scarcely repress a smile on reading these words, as it occurred to my mind that this was a sly joke of the worthy governor's on the desirability – from the official

point of view – of the rapid emigration of paupers to Spirit Land.

Christmas, it appears, had been the sole theme of conversation for months previous to my arrival, and various were the surmises as to how it would pass off. 'I wish it was Christmas tomorrow, for I ain't hed a feed for six months, and I cud do we a buster now.' 'I ain't hed nowt to eat wuth a menshun sin I've bin in.' 'And I ain't either, and am longing for a bit o' bacca.' 'Roll on a pound o' plum duff, six ounce o' roast beef, a nounce o' bacca, and a pint of ale, and I shell last for a nuther twelve munth.' These and similar expressions are continually heard months before the great Feed arrives. Who can wonder, when one considers the paltry and insignificant amount of food which is doled out to the inmates? Even those Nottingham slaves who may be seen daily dragging a load of firewood, the weight of which, together with the cart, is equal to nearly half a ton, receive not an atom of extra food beyond the regular six ounces of bread and tin of skilly, morning and night. On Monday an extraordinary repast is provided for dinner, consisting of three ounces of bread and a tin of veritable dish-washings. In fact a candle stirred in a pot of boiling water would be far preferable to the swill served out as nourishing broth. On Tuesday and Thursday the dinner diet is four ounces of meat(?) with potatoes boiled in their jackets. Fish was served every Thursday until the authorities saw that the inmates would rather 'clam' than eat it. This was no fault of the fish, as it was generally sound enough, but the manner of cooking and serving rendered it uneatable, even by the half-starved paupers.

Just fancy a whole head, with the gaping jaws and the glaring eye sockets, put upon one plate, the tail deposited on another, and a sickly admixture of flour and water poured over each mess. Instead of being eaten, the fish was often arranged into various devices on the plates. The tail of a finny 'un might be inserted

into its jaws, and the whole deposited on a pedestal of the bones, presenting a curious spectacle to those officials who went through the dining hall after a fish dinner. On Monday the gigantic feast of three ounces of bread with a tin of pea soup is provided for the mid-day meal. On Fridays, the inmates luxuriate on a pound of pudding, with a sauce not unlike neatsfoot oil, seasoned with a little vinegar and sugar. On Saturdays a small quantity of Irish stew forms the extravagant repast.

Do not, therefore, wonder that the inmates look forward to the Christmas 'gorge' with the pleasure of hope, knowing that for once in the year the gnawing worm in their stomachs is likely to be stilled. The happy day at length arrives, and the breakfast for this eventful morning is more attractive to the skilly 'gorgers', as they receive tea instead of gruel, and are even presented with a quarter of an ounce of butter to their six-ounce 'cracker', morning and night. After breakfast, divine service is held in the dinner hall, which in its ordinary state is a cold, cheerless, dark looking room that strikes a chill to the very bones as you enter it from the warm wards. It is certain that many a poor old man has had his days curtailed by having to get his food in such a damp and draughty place. On this occasion, however, what a contrast is presented! Festoons of evergreens hang around, stars and other devices occupy the vacant spaces, the long, bare gas pendants are dressed in an attractive manner - in fact the whole room is handsomely decorated. The chill even seems to be taken away, and a general warmth prevails.

Towards noon, visitors begin to arrive, for the express purpose of seeing the 'animals feed', and various are the comments heard, as to the extraordinary comforts provided for the pauper. These people only see the workhouse in its holiday attire, and are apt to be led astray by the apparent comfort, and even luxury, which the pauper enjoys. Superficial observers are likely to din into the ears of any poor creature who may apply

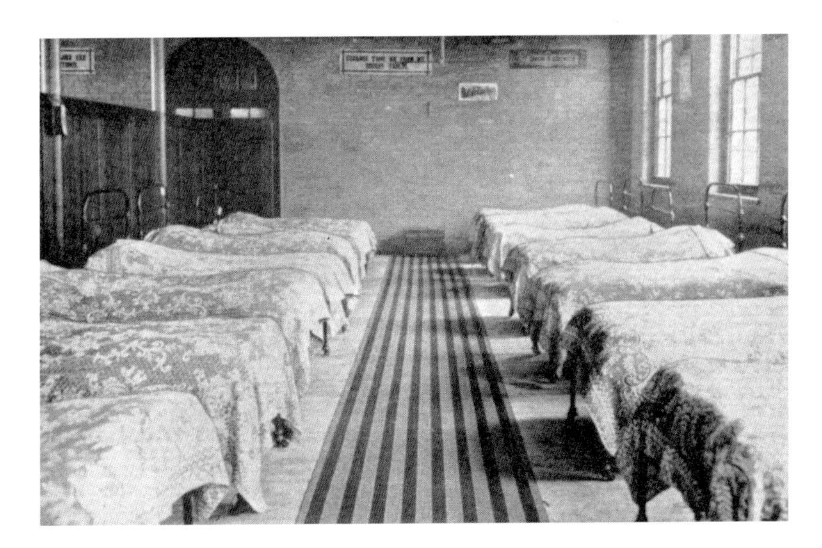

Scenes in the Gordon Memorial Home – spartan, but doubtless a great deal more comfortable than the streets.

to them for relief the well-known phrase: 'Go to the workhouse, you will be well cared for there.' In this case there are two sides to the picture, and I beg ratepapers who have looked only on the holiday side to take an opportunity of also examining the everyday reverse. Christmas Day is misleading, and so also are such days as those of Councillor Gregory's treat.

At last the dinner bell sounds and a general stampede commences towards the hall. Never, except on this and similar occasions, is there such a unanimous desire to enter the room. On the extreme right, as you enter the hall, are seated the young women, and to the left of them the old ladies in their snowy caps. The centre is occupied by the old gentlemen, attired on this occasion in their Sunday best. On the extreme left are ranged the young and able-bodied men, who with appetites keenly whetted, anxiously await the moment of attack, sniffing with evident delight the fumes of approaching roast beef.

Immediately grace is said, up fly four sliding doors, and the steaming edibles are carried by active paupers of both sexes to their respective contingents. Of course, the old ladies and gentlemen are first served, then the hungry young ones come in for their share. The six ounces of – for once – good roast beef, garnished with potatoes ready peeled, are supplied to each inmate. This allowance is soon demolished by the voracious able bodied, and the clatter of their knives and forks is stilled long before the old men have got through their job. Anxious glances are turned towards the sliding doors for the plum duff and coveted pint of ale (which latter would be debarred altogether if 'Windbag and Water-Melon' could have his way). Eventually, the efforts of the attacking force are relaxed, their faces look flushed, and they appear different individuals altogether.

Pieces of paper, pocket handerchiefs and other wrappers are now produced for the purpose of gathering up the fragments

of the repast, which are duly deposited in the solitary pocket I have described for future use. The pint of ale is drained, tobacco is served to the men, tea and sugar to the women, buns, oranges, sweets and so on to the children, and in about an hour from the commencement of the charge the battle is over. A member of the board arises and makes a 'few remarks' about as edifying as Maccabe's celebrated after-dinner speech. Then, after wishing all a Merry Christmas and a Happy New Year, a general exodus is made from the hall to the various wards, the young men shouting out: 'Roll on, next Christmas, for another feed.' In the evening divine service is again held, at which the harmony of Mr Copleston's choir is very welcome. Service over, the inmates again retire to their various wards and fight the day's battle o'er again. A little extra indulgence is granted on this occasion, and instead of all being in bed 'like good children' by eight o'clock, it is drawing towards ten before an ascent is made to the men's attic.

This retreat is a special feature of the house. It is a long room formed by the sloping of the roof. Innumerable baulks and supports intercept you at every few feet, and about eighty beds are generally occupied, about Christmas time, in that roosting place. The bedsteads are placed in every conceivable position, head to foot, side to head and so on, throughout its length and breadth, forming such a labyrinth that the poor old men who occupy a room at each end of the attic often get lost and scrape their poor old shins when they have to grope their way in the darkness. Economy forbids the use of a light except in the hospital or on the staircases.

Well, the reader can form some idea what a Babel of tongues is heard in the attic on this occasion, when the pint of ale has greased them. Comic songs and tales are sung and related, and occasional barking, mewing, crowing, and every conceivable kind of noise add to the general hubbub. All the hawkers' cries – 'Tops, swede tops', 'Watercresses', 'Peas and

Sausage', 'Salt' – and all the well known street cries are bellowed out with such lustiness as would make you fancy that the residents of Woodborough Road or York Street would not be able to sleep. 'Roll on, Walter Gregory's treat,' one will shout. 'I think it's cowd on that this year,' another will respond. 'Well, then, roll on, Jubilee, we shall get a feed then.' These and other larks are kept up till the midnight hour has chimed, and at length Morpheus claims his subjects one by one, until his hand closes the lips and eyes of the last of the yarning Mohicans.

from

The Man Who Worked On Sundays

REVD LESLIE SKINNER

Leslie Skinner was chaplain to the Eighth (Independent) Armoured Brigade attached to the Sherwood Rangers Yeomanry Regiment during the Second World War. In recent years he has published his personal war diary of the year between June

1944 and May 1945, and the Christmas in the middle of that period saw him and his brigade in Belgium. Not far away, German divisions were on the move, some heading for Liège and others expecting to try to drive through to Antwerp, and the brigade was in a high state of readiness in anticipation of this latter offensive. Nevertheless, Christmas passed peacefully, apart from a skirmish of the musical kind.

Sunday, 24 December

Busy day. Brigade orchestra had been very good at Sherwood Rangers Yeomanry morning service (attended by 200). Hard work elsewhere, with no music available. Following brief stand-to in evening, a local brass band concert, and I had to lead carol singing – heavy going. A chap from Amsterdam, said to be Jewish, sang a propaganda song in Dutch with eleven verses, to tune of *Silver Threads among the Gold.* Frenchy's batman also sang. A saxophone soloist had argument in middle with pianist as to which bar he had to play next!!!

Monday, 25 December

Goodish mail – two letters from Etta, tobacco from her dad.

09.00 Christmas Communion SRY – 22 present.

10.00 Brigade HQ Service, 45 present and 11 Holy Communion. No band – brigadier bit annoyed. Went OK.

I remember that the service had to be in the same room where troops' Christmas lunch was to be served. Tables laid out on three sides of room and the 'congregation' sitting inside the square. Cook had prepared a splendid boar's head with orange in its mouth. I had to preach across the top table with brigadier six feet from me and the boar's head between us. Disconcerting till I saw funny side of it.

11.15 Service with Company – 40 present and 14 Holy Communion. No music.

Back to Regiment in time for lunch – helped to wait on the men with other officers at HQ, with A Squadron and LAD combined. Fairly quiet afternoon. Stand-to after tea as usual. Regimental officers' cocktail party in evening. Dinner quite good. Finished up at A Squadron and then to bed, rather late and very tired. At cocktail party Derek Warwick, Sherwood Rangers Yeomanry officer with 21 Army Group, made draw for officers' home leave. Smith first and Hylda second.

Tuesday, 26 December

Morning chasing 12 Corps rear HQ – moved location. Wanting information re. my home leave situation for Etta – she will want to know. No luck. In afternoon regimental children's party – 50 invited or expected and around 250 turned up, as whole families came. Neville Fearn as Father Christmas and George Culley as clown arrived on sledge drawn by light tank – absolutely great do. Moving tomorrow. Wrote Etta.

Christmas Seventy Years Ago

NEVILLE BINGHAM

Neville Bingham was born in 1915 and lived all his life in Main Street, Sutton-on-Trent, where he died in 1990. Much loved as a farmer, a collector of domestic and agricultural artefacts and a speaker who could pack meetings of the local history society, he left several fragments of biography which he had intended to edit and refine. Three of them, on the Main Street, Wartime Sutton and this Christmas recollection, were published in the early 1990s in aid of chapel and church funds.

It was almost Christmas time when the first part of this book was completed, when one of my grandchildren said to me one day: 'What was Christmas like when you were a boy, Grandpa?' Christmas was different between then and now. For instance, we had no laid-on water in the house, so we had to go to the pump or well outside the house or down the garden. You had little hot water in the house except the side boiler, which was part of the cooking range. If that was not sufficient you had to keep the kettle boiling over the open fire.

There was no electricity in the village, so there was very little lighting in the house except the one double-burner oil lamp placed in the centre of the table on a winter's night; and

it was always a candle to light you to bed, instead of flicking a light switch as you go upstairs. The village streets were very dark to travel about, so people used to carry their hurricane lamps – or candle lamps, which often blew out. If we had a lovely moon at Christmas time it was much appreciated by everyone. If the streets were as dark today, no one would now venture out for fear of their lives.

Then, of course, we had no telephone, so we could not ring our relatives or friends to give them the season's greetings. I can remember the first telegraph office being installed in our local Post Office, and if you wanted to send a message to anyone in the country you had to write out the message on a form, and they would transmit the message to the exchange in the nearest town or village. The telegram would be delivered by a telegraph boy dressed in Post Office uniform.

About this time, also, the Royal Mail was a haphazard delivery. All our local mail had to be taken to Newark Post Office, and the mail for distribution in Sutton brought back. Herbert Rushby used to do this work when he was a youth, travelling to Newark and back on his cycle. Except for a period during the First World War, he spent all his working life in the postal service, starting with a cycle and ending with a mail van.

Another thing we did not have was wireless and television. The first wireless set we had was a crystal set, and as it only had a pair of earphones only one could listen at a time. What did we have? We had some jolly good Christmases. You see, we had to make them. Christmas never comes to anyone. You have to go out of your way and get it, and you will not do this by sitting in a chair looking at television all day. Most of our entertainment came from around the piano. There was always someone in the house who could play, so all of us used to gather around singing and making as much noise as possible. Then, when you got fed up or exhausted, you had the old

The band outside Boots, a once familiar picture in the Nottingham-based chemist chain's shops.

wind-up gramophone squeaking out 'Just a Song at Twilight' or 'Home Sweet Home'.

The preparation for Christmas did not really commence until Advent, or the first week of December, with the exception perhaps of the making of the Christmas cake and plum pudding. When these were being prepared, then everyone would join in to have a stir of the ingredients. At the same time you had a wish. It was considered good luck, too, when this duty was performed. Then the plum pudding would be steamed for at least eight hours. Many people used to boil their puddings in the wash copper, but this was a practice we never followed, as it was likely to get too much water inside the basin, so the puddings tasted somewhat wet and soggy. Steamed gently for many hours, they tasted perfect. Not many people make their own Christmas puddings today, as it is considered uneconomical. You can buy a proprietary brand equally good. When the Christmas pudding was being served, we would scrutinize the outer part carefully to see if we could find out where the silver threepenny bits had been placed. It was always the custom to put them in, as silver did not contaminate the pudding in any way. Sometimes we were lucky and sometimes not, and if there were fourteen of us round the table on Christmas Day, which there usually were, then quite a few of us were unlucky.

We felt the approach of Christmas when the posters went up announcing the Fur and Feather Whist Drive, where most folk used to try and win their Christmas dinner. The first prize usually was a goose, the second prize either a duck or a stag and the third prize a rabbit. For the uninitiated, a stag was a farmyard cockerel. All these prizes would be undressed – that is, in their feathers or fur – so there was still work to do after you had won something. But no one minded this, because you had got your dinner. We usually had two geese for Christmas Day, and it was always my lot to pluck and

draw these birds for the oven. One goose, if it was well fed, would serve eight people for a meal, so having folk in, we usually cooked two. On Boxing Day we had a large piece of beef.

It was a great advantage to us that we did most of the cooking in the bakehouse oven, which was still hot enough to cook on Christmas Day, owing to late baking on Christmas Eve. Many of the village people often brought their large joints and poultry for us to bake for them. Often their cottage ovens were too small for that purpose. We baked all their pork pies when they killed a pig, and I have seen a time when you could hardly put your foot down for fear of treading on uncooked pork pies waiting to go into the oven. Each had its own trade mark for identification purposes. These hand-raised pork pies were made on wooden moulds, bound round with newspaper and then fastened securely with two dressmaking pins, to stop them collapsing on baking. We often had 'tired' pies, as we called them – pies that started to sit down before they went into the oven; but nothing could be done about this, because we only baked them. After the baking we used to rip all the papers off whilst still warm, sweep all the papers and pins up, and burn the lot in the flue straight away. I remember once, after this operation, a man came to ask if he could have his pins back. We told him yes, if he would care to extract them from the flue.

We saved all the feathers from the poultry plucking. These were sorted into various categories. Goose and duck down went for making feather beds. It was customary then for a daughter to receive a feather bed from her parents as a wedding present. Geese and duck wings were cut off at the first joint and kept for cleaning flues, or places where a brush could not reach. Under beds to clean the springs, for instance; they were very useful for that purpose. The coarser feathers went to make pillows and cushions.

When anyone had saved enough feathers to make either pillows or feather beds, they would often send them to our bakehouse to be 'stoved'. This was a process used to kill any fleas or creepy-crawlies which lived on poultry. So these packs would be put into the ovens last thing at night, left until morning and then taken out before the fire was lit.

'Did you believe in Santa Claus?' I was asked. Of course we did, so we hung our stockings up in anticipation, the same as you do today. Mind you, we did not get much left in them; a few nuts in the toe of the stocking and probably a silver coin, followed by an orange or an apple, a few sweets, then probably something useful like a pair of socks or a tie or a handkerchief. This was a sample of things that Santa left us, and never once can I remember his leaving me a toy of any kind. Of course there were toys, mostly made of wood, like a Noah's Ark set and farmyard animals, wooden engines and wheelbarrows. You see, there were too many of us for any of these things, as money was so scare. A good table was all that mattered, so we never grumbled about it because we knew we should be having some real fun later on by playing games.

Whilst television dominates Christmas today, our festivities were more active through playing games. Believe me, some of these were quite hilarious. At any gathering we went to there were always some clowns who got the party going. Let me tell you about some of the games we played. No party was complete without playing Postman's Knock, when one member went outside the door whilst the remainder were given numbers. Then, after the given signal, he would knock on the door saying he had a letter for number so and so. This number would then go out and duly receive the reward of a kiss, and then stay out to be the Postman. Many a romance started in that way.

Another game we played which caused great amusement was Passing the Message. All the players would stand in a

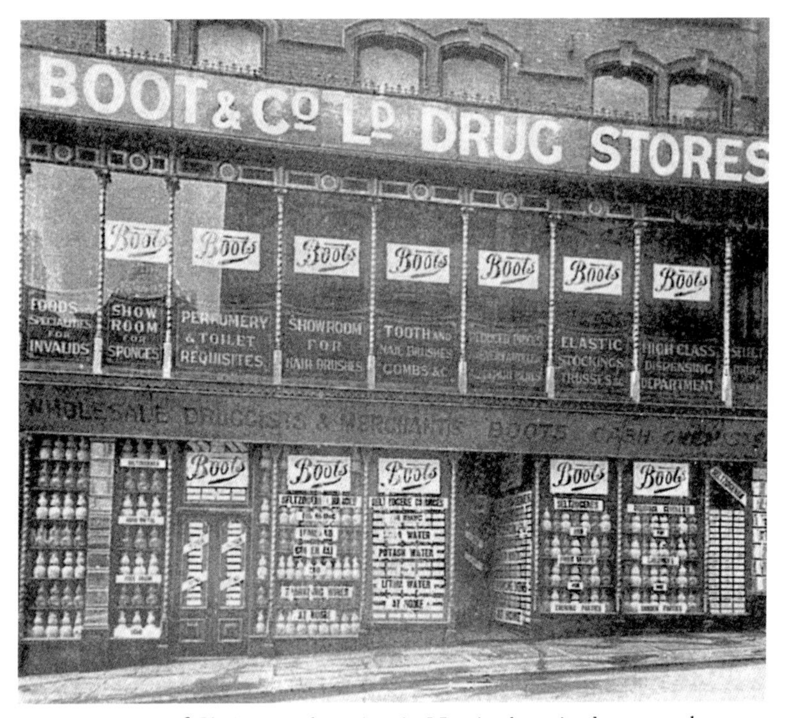

Memories of Christmas shopping in Nottingham in days gone by. Opposite: Beecroft's toyshop, seen here in late Victorian times, served a generation. Above: Jesse Boot's great new store of the 1880s.

line across the room. The leader then whispered a message in the ear of the first person and he would pass on the message he had received to his neighbour and so on, till the end of the line. This last person would tell all the room the message he had received. This invariably would end up very different from the original one. For example, the first person's message 'Mrs Smith has bought some kippers' could well come out as 'Mrs Smith has wet her knickers', or sometimes much worse.

Presents! Presents!

NOTTINGHAM EXCHANGE.

When we were boys,
We bought our Toys
at
BEECROFT'S.

Now we are men,
We'll go again
to
BEECROFT'S.

For all the Latest Novelties in

TOYS,

GAMES AND FANCY GOODS

GO TO

Beecroft & Sons, Exchange Corner,

MARKET PLACE, NOTTINGHAM.

No party would be complete without the game of Murder. This, to be played properly, needed the run of the whole house in darkness to create the right atmosphere. Playing cards were needed to select who the detectives were to be. Whoever had the ace of spades was to be the murderer, but he had not to let on he had this card. That was for the detectives to find out after the murder had been committed. You can imagine the fun created by this game, the squealing and rattling of chamber pots under the beds, and the piercing shrieks of the person being murdered.

After this a quieter game would often be suggested, like Finding the Ring. The competitors would form a circle around a circle of string which had a brass ring threaded on. Everybody had to make the motion of passing the ring on, and the one in the middle had to watch carefully to see if he could spot who had it. If he was successful then the one who was caught with it had to go in the centre.

Left and opposite: exterior and interior views of the ancient Trip to Jerusalem in Nottingham in the inter-war years, a marvellously atmospheric pub at this time of year.

A rather eerie and gruesome game was Ghost Story. All sat round the table with their hands on the top. All lights were put out, and then someone would make up a ghostly murder story. To make it become real, somewhat suspect articles would be passed round as the story unfolded – a chicken's gizzard for the heart, pigs' eyes and tails, rattling chains and slippery ice cubes. This was a very merry but gruesome game, and if you had someone who could spin a good murder yarn then it was horrendous.

After a game like this, we would opt for a quieter one like 'Mrs McKenzie has died. How did she die?' The reply from your neighbour might be 'with her eyes shut', and everyone would shut their eyes. The game would proceed round the

room with everybody making additions until the competitors looked like contortionists.

Another energetic game we played was called Stations. Everybody had the name of a station. The one in the centre would call out two station names, and then these two would have to exchange places before the centre person could get to one or other of them first. When it came to 'All Change', then everybody had to move, which made it easier for the one in the middle.

Honeymoon Rush was another popular game. Two people, one lady and one gent, came into the room with a portmanteau full of clothes, which they had to put on above their own. This game was timed, and the winners were the ones who donned all the clothes in the shortest time. No party was complete without Charades, and invariably this game was the climax to the evening. It also entailed dressing up, and the object of the game was to guess the theme the players had thought of. This could be done by acting one or two scenes to bring in the full title.

There was any number of parties going on at Christmas. and we received many invitations. It was this sort of thing we looked forward to rather than what we received in our stocking; the joy and merriment we created was our reward. We did not care how far we went to a party, and walking was often the only means. I remember our family had been invited to a Christmas party at a house on Grassthorpe Hill. A family by the name of Wallers lived there, and we went to school with their children Norah, Phyllis and Jack. Jack was my own age. We walked to this party, while at ten o'clock, outside the house waiting to bring us home, was Charlie Skelton's carrier's van drawn by two grey horses. Today, if you had no motor car or a lift of some kind, you would not bother to go. Christmas finished in my days, as it does today, on Twelfth Night, and usually on this night we had a visit from the

village mummers acting the Plough Monday play. They would do this for a bit of beer money. I can remember four of the team by name – Tibby Walster, Charlie Clay, and two of the Parkinson brothers, Kel and Tuckman. All the Parkinson boys had nicknames, the other two being Tot and Toby. They all lived in a cottage down the Church Walk, now pulled down. After Plough Monday, the real finish of Christmas, the village settled down to its usual routine.

Yuletide in Bygone Days

S. JACKSON COLEMAN

This brief piece comes from Quaint Lore of Nottinghamshire, *published several years ago by barrister S. Jackson Coleman in a pamphlet produced by the Folklore Fellowship.*

Old-time Christmas festivities in Nottinghamshire included many quaint customs which are seldom seen nowadays. It was customary, for instance, to toast apples on a string until they dropped into a bowl of highly spiced ale that had been placed to receive them. This, from the softness of the beverage, was called 'Lamb's Wool'. There are yet a few who can recall the

'hoodeners' with the *Owd 'Oss*. This 'horse' was constructed of a broom handle with the crude carving of a horse's head stuck on the top, with a moveable jaw or clapper which one lad worked. He was covered over with an old rug or jacket – mostly a worn-out cart rug. The rattling of a money box was accompanied with the chanting of a doggerel which began:

> This is a poor old horse,
> Who's carried me many a mile,
> O'er hedges and ditches and many a crooked mile.

Death at Christmas

RAY GOSLING

A very different view of Christmas from Ray Gosling, the quirky Nottingham-born broadcaster and writer. It comes from his memoir of the Sixties, Personal Copy, *published by Faber and Faber in 1980, and captures a period of his life when he led a double existence, as an increasingly familiar television face and as the chairman of a large tenants' and residents' association in an inner-city district of Nottingham. The Christmas recalled here was a time when it was difficult to reconcile the two roles.*

I could go on about the nitty-gritty of housing and back-street/council-house life. Maybe I should. But that makes

another book – maybe that *is* the book, but it's not how this book began and there were other things in my life. In 1972 I was making films about places for television. In December I was preparing my commentary for a film about Rochdale – running into the very last days of editing, trying to wheedle into the script everything I wanted to say.

Rochdale is an interesting town: begetter of the Co-Op, drab and wet and its people over-friendly but ever so interesting to me because in the cotton mills – they still have them – there are thousands of immigrants working. Ukranians, Filipino girls on contract labour and the Pakistanis – all Muslims. Now I always thought when I was young the immigrants would make an *England Half-English*, which is the title of a collection of essays by my mentor, Colin MacInnes. I thought the immigrants would bring calypso bands and colour and freedom and life to our drab industrial towns. It hasn't happened like that in Rochdale. As the native English Nonconformist has faded away, these new arrivals have come along and, particularly the Muslim immigrants, have brought it all back. The spirit of my father. The spirit of hard work, abstemiousness and self-sufficiency. Don't drink. Don't smoke. Don't kiss in the street. Don't marry unless your father approves.

You'd think the children of immigrant parents, Muslim boys and girls born in Rochdale, might rebel like I did – or be corrupted by our now permissive English ways – but I found they were not. I met Pakistani schoolgirls spoken for. Ukranian teenagers believing in a strict and moral life. I do envy the immigrants their industriousness. I'm glad I wasn't a child of theirs and I fear for our permissive society.

I'm writing this at home (in Nottingham), trying to wangle it into the script in as few words as the pictures will let me. It's not the way to make films. It's not the way I'd like it. I go up to the studios on the train and try to lengthen the picture,

then come back home and play with the words. Put away the script for a long weekend of neighbourhood politics, seeing people, of sitting in our community shop taking up the complaints. I did the Saturday morning session. There was a meeting on Sunday. I should have gone there on Monday to talk to Arthur, now secretary, about future moves. I didn't. And on Tuesday morning I learnt on the telephone that Arthur had collapsed, after doing a session at the shop. The Catholic priest had picked him up off the street and he was taken to hospital. I phoned the town clerk to forward all business to me, and then I phoned the hospital. It was clearly serious. They said visitors apart from kin were not allowed. I worked on the Rochdale script, and an article I was preparing on dog racing. But every time I left my desk to make a cup of tea, I swelled up inside, all my senses tense, and yet I slept okay that night.

Wednesday, 20 December

The phone rang at seven a.m. I was half awake when Trevor, his son-in-law, said he had died. So many to tell, said Trevor, so much to do. He was such a wonderful man, wonderful man – never be another – could I meet the family in the afternoon to talk about the arrangements? I re-dialled, passing the message on to Margaret, our community girl, that Arthur was dead. She burst into an uncontrollable sob. I just put the phone down. Got dressed. Made a cup of coffee. Worked on the Rochdale script.

When a friend is ill, like yesterday, I wanted to tell the world and get everyone to pray, that was the implication. But now Arthur's dead I want to tell no one. I want to pretend it hasn't happened. It helps, having to concentrate on other things, being much too busy with work.

At nine o'clock the phone went again. There was big trouble. Every year we gave free Christmas parcels to our old

folk. This year some had got two and some had got none. The old folks were scrapping, and how's Arthur? He's dead, in the night. Oh God! Now about these Christmas parcels . . . You can't believe it, at ten o'clock there's more phone calls coming in. There's going to be such a fuss at the passing of Arthur. Almost a competition for the best displays of grief and, in the midst of our grief, Sid is calling for an emergency meeting. What an insult to Arthur who built us up, that we're not strong enough to calmly continue. Still, we're a family business, but I wish we'd mourned first before plotting who is to fill Arthur's shoes. I've just had a terrible thought – what if the hippies had pushed Arthur down, or the blacks? Folk are only a degree from wanting to avenge this death. None of us expected it, and now I've heard there's to be a post-mortem. Apparently it's normal when a man dies suddenly to have a post-mortem. But what food that gives to rumour.

At three o'clock I went down to meet the family. They'd a handful of things that'd been in Arthur's pocket when he fell: papers, a new diary for 1973, meetings already pencilled in. I'd take some of the papers – to do with the small shops question, his great campaign to get new corner shops built. The family asked me – because I am a writer, aren't I – to concoct the memorial for the local paper's death column. For a moment I thought of being original but somehow it wasn't the time. We got some old newspapers and I read out loud what others had put in for theirs, and then we copied down the phrases we liked: 'patiently borne' – that's nice – 'united with mother and baby', 'passed away sudden' – you can't say died. 'Never to be forgotten', 'he left without a last goodbye' – trite? True.

The widow seemed sprightly, but the grandchildren, they weep, the young uncontrollable as we hammer out the arrangements. There will be a lying-in at the undertaker's, and the Tenants' Association will provide pallbearers. Two of

us will ride in the family car. How about flowers? Who's going to make them over Christmas? Florists will all be shut, and we've got to have flowers. I tell them I'll see Derek. Our street stewards convener, he's got a grocer's shop with market connections. Leave it to me. The widow insists the family pay for all the notices in the paper, so there's a great reckoning up and sorting out of small change. 'He was always straight, Arthur, he'd have wished it – now how much do I owe you if you take the notice to the paper for us?' It's a comfort, oddly, being penny-minded and small-change prudent in this storm; but the grandchildren, how they cried. Why are the young closer to death?

We have too many wanting to be pallbearers. I suppose we'll have to draw lots. One of the weeping grandchildren leaves the house to walk off into the derelict, and she gets lost. A search party goes out for her, torches in the dark. I leave them – sleep on the train Manchester-bound again.

Thursday, 21 December

Straight into the studio this morning without going to my office. We record the commentary, first take. I leave without going to the canteen. Speak to no one, coffee from a corridor machine and taxi back to the station. Train and sleep. They want the bit on dog racing more quickly. What shall I do about Christmas?

Friday, 22 December

A meeting last night in a room above the local pub. A Labour Party politician said you can't have a tenants' association without a secretary. Call an emergency meeting. I will not. In the upstairs room it's counselling time with three families left holding out on rent strike. Against the Fair Rent increase for council-house tenants. We organized a rent strike in the summer, everybody was with us. Say no, mass meetings,

lobbies and leaflets. The doubters said – everyone'll pay in the end. They were right. Here are the last three telling me: I would carry on not paying, but it's the wife you see, she worries about eviction so we've got to pay, haven't we? The last three resisters are not lefties at all. They're quiet and determined, puritan-proud rather than socialist families. Arthur would have liked them. No boozy talk here, but sober determination not to pay simply because they have no right of appeal against an arbitrary increase. It isn't fair. They're right. We've lost.

Saturday, 23 December

And it goes on and on. Christmas is coming and I haven't got a chance. I'm doing the complaints bureau down at the shop when the chairman of a new Labour city council committee calls. Can I prepare a report on the need for community facilities for a special meeting the council have for the 28th? That's the day of Arthur's funeral – Christmas is gone. If I do a good report we stand a chance of getting a permanent headquarters. I cancel all the plans I had for seeing my mother and father at Christmas.

Tuesday, 26 December

It's been a nice Christmas. John came home unexpectedly in a taxi on Christmas Day from Los Angeles. Friends came round to eat. I slept a lot.

Wednesday, 27 December

On Boxing Day I took the dogs for a walk, to talk to people about Arthur. Today I've been to see him, viewing they call it, at the lying-in at the undertaker's. The rooms were lined with wood like ships. I've come to see Mr Leatherland, I said, and a prim lady through a little hatch in the panelled wood said: 'Take a seat for a moment, would you, please?'

The undertaker's smelt very nice, a cross between a florist's and a curry shop. Arthur lay in the coffin. You could see the bruises on his face where he fell. He was surprisingly small and still with his eyes closed. I prayed to God, demanding he bring Arthur back, to let his keen eyes open and sort out this Christmas parcel wrangle.

There was a meeting to work out pallbearers. It was surprisingly calm. Derek had organized the wreaths. Sid had six black armbands for all the bearers, the cars had been told to drive slowly through the streets and the vicar, though a new man, would do the service appropriately. Walking home I said to myself, he's dead, all dead and gone. Let's bury the dead and be done.

Doles and Confects

CORNELIUS BROWN

These two stories come from the splendid Notes about Notts: A Collection of Singular Sayings, Curious Customs, Eccentric Epitaphs and Interesting Items *published by Forman's of Long Row, Nottingham in 1874. It is typical of such rag-bags of folk tales, full of such qualifying phrases as 'tradition has it' and 'it is said'. Mayor Carruthers, who repaired the town pumps instead of sending cakes to the big-wigs, was a civic dignitary of whom even the satirical magazine* The Owl *would have approved.*

Christmas Doles – an Interesting Story

In 1735 the Leakes of Sutton were in the habit of distributing dole loaves to the poor of the neighbourhood. Captain Waterhouse relates an interesting story in connection with this custom. He says: 'one of the Leakes, doughty knight, Sir Nicholas, carried away by the prevailing enthusiasm of his day, became, as was then the fashion, a crusader; and, as a pledge, broke a ring with his dame. Poor man, it became, as the sequel will show, the bond of a happy reunion, and formed a quaintly pretty incident.

'In the varying fortune of war he was taken prisoner by the Turks, and kept in close confinement; his owner, believing him to be of noble extraction, considered his captive valuable as a means to extort ransom. After lying in prison for several years, without the least hope of being released, he prayed to the Almighty to grant him the favour of seeing Sutton once more – making a vow that if the favour were granted, in gratitude to God, he would leave a bequest to the poor for ever. Tradition goes on to say that Sir Nicholas at length lived to find, unknown to himself, that he was within the porch of Sutton church. As his memory returned, and he recognized the place, he asked of the retainers if the lady of the house was yet living.

'Being informed that she was on that day occupied in bestowing a dole, as in affectionate remembrance of her lost lord, he made speedy application to speak to her. She, understanding what a miserable garb and condition the strange supplicant was in, declined to grant the request, but desired him to be relieved at the gate. He then sent her the half ring, which she compared with her own; the parts coinciding, she recognized and acknowledged her long mourned lord, and cherished him until the way-worn pilgrim recovered his health and strength. So he devised eight bushels of wheat to be baked into loaves, and given to the poor of Sutton, Duckmanton and Normanton on St Nicholas' day for ever.'

A Christmas Custom

At Christmas the Mayor of Nottingham used to send cakes (confects) to his friends. The custom was broken in upon by Mr Carruthers, and never renewed. He, instead, repaired the town pumps, and the relation of the fact was for some time on a brass plate on the pump at Weekday Cross. The pumps stood where the old crosses and conduits had been, at Butter Cross, Weekday Cross, one at the House of Correction, where the Templars had a house, one at the Swan, where the Whitefriars had another, one at the end of Broad Marsh, where the Greyfriars had another, one at the entrance of Roper's Close, and one just outside of Chapel Bar.

Storm Clouds of War

ALFRED C. WOOD

Newark for the royalists, Nottingham for the roundheads. The north–south split of the county is well documented – and it was at and around Christmas 1642 that events dictated the course of those divided loyalties. Alfred C. Wood's account of the age-old animosity, Nottinghamshire in the Civil War, *was published in 1937.*

When the Edgehill campaign was over, Sir John Digby returned to the county with the intention of securing it for the king. Such a coup was imperative if the royalist cause was to be maintained in the area, for Lincolnshire was predominantly parliamentarian in sympathy, and in October Sir John Gell had mastered Derbyshire and occupied Derby for the two houses. To achieve his purpose, Digby summoned all the justices of the shire to meet him at the Talbot Inn, Newark on 10 December.

The alleged object of this assembly was to confer of such things as might best lead to 'the defence of our county and safety of our persons and estates', but the sheriff had raised a force of eighty horse, and if Mrs Hutchinson can be believed, he intended to seize those whose roundhead inclinations were notorious at the Newark conference, and then secure Nottingham with his troops for the king. John Hutchinson and Francis

A vintage picture of the bedroom at the Saracen's Head in Southwell where Charles I stayed in May 1646, after surrendering to the Scots.

Pierrepont were among those summoned, but they were warned of Digby's intended treachery and excused themselves. Hutchinson promptly advised the town of Nottingham of its projected occupation by the royalists, and the inhabitants, having already endured one prolonged experience of the plundering proclivities of the cavalier troops, readily agreed to defend themselves against any force sent to seize the town. About seven hundred men were hurriedly enlisted and George Hutchinson, John's brother, who had lived in Nottingham and was well known and esteemed there, was chosen to command them.

In face of such preparations, the sheriff dared enter the county town. Instead, efforts were made to negotiate, and for a fortnight letters passed between the two camps with assurances of peaceful intentions which hardly veiled the underlying suspicions of each other's motives. Lord Chaworth, Sir Thomas Williamson of East Markham, Sir Matthew Palmer of Southwell, Sir Roger Cooper of Thurgarton, Sir Gervase Eyre of Rampton, Robert Sutton of Averham and John Millington from Sturton, who were all with Digby in Newark, wrote to Hutchinson and Pierrepont with apparent sincerity, urging a meeting, and it was at length arranged to take place 'at a village in the country on the forest side', on 24 December. Hutchinson attended, only to find that none of the royalists had arived. They excused themselves on the grounds that they had received his acceptance too late to enable them to turn up in time, and proposed a new appointment as soon as Christmas was over.

But by then the chasm had opened too wide for fair words to bridge, and the resolution of both sides was stiffening. The spirits of the royalist gentry in Newark had been heightened by the arrival between 18 and 23 December of about four thousand horse sent by the Earl of Newcastle, whom Charles had left in command of all his forces in the North. Early in

December the earl marched south from Newcastle, where he had collected his army, and occupied York. A few days later he routed Lord Fairfax, the parliamentary general in Yorkshire, at Tadcaster, and established himself at Pontefract, where he severed all communications between Hull, still held for parliament by Sir John Hotham, and the clothing towns of the West Riding, all of which were in parliamentary hands.

From here he promptly dispatched Sir John Henderson in command of a large party of horse to support Digby in holding Newark, the strategic value of which he was quick to recognize. Commanding the lowest bridge over the Trent and standing on the main road south, it was the funnel through which any invasion of parliament's territory from the north must pour; its possession ensured an indispensable link with the king's head-quarters at Oxford; it formed a rallying point for the hitherto unorganized loyalty of Nottinghamshire, and at the same time bridled the activities of the parliamentarians in Lincolnshire; it would provide a valuable bulwark against any attack upon the king's northern territory. Lying at the tip of that great wedge of royalist country which ran down between Lincolnshire on the one hand and the Yorkshire cloth towns and Derbyshire on the other hand, its strategic value, either for offensive or defensive purposes, was enormous; and as its later history proved, Sir John Digby and the earl served their master well when they secured for him the old market town and its wooden bridges.

Sir John Henderson at once began to throw up earthworks to fortify the place, and wrote urging Newcastle to send more troops so that he might occupy Grantham and Belvoir. The latter belonged to the Earl of Rutland, who was a supporter of parliament; but he was not in residence, and before January was out Lord Camden, Colonel Gervase Lucas and others had secured it for the king. During the remainder of the war it played an important part as one of the satellite garrisons of

Newark. The same month Colonel Henry Hastings, second son of the Earl of Huntingdon, who had raised forces for Charles in Leicestershire, planted a garrison on the banks of the Trent at Wilden or Wilne Ferry – now Cavendish Bridge – and held fast in spite of the efforts of Sir John Gell to dislodge him from a position which menaced the parliamentarians both in Derbyshire and at Nottingham. In February the counties of Leicester, Derby, Nottingham, Lincoln, and Rutland were associated by the king's order, and Hastings was made colonel-general of all the royalist forces in them.

All this weakened any inclination which the cavaliers at Newark might have had towards neutrality and peace, and the parliamentarians in Nottingham were by now equally forward in their preparations for war. On December 15 the two houses passed an ordinance which associated the eight counties of Buckingham, Bedford, Northampton, Huntingdon, Rutland, Leicester, Derby, and Nottingham for their mutual defence, and committees were appointed in each of the shires to raise men, horses, arms, and money – the last of which was to be repaid with eight per cent interest. Thomas, Lord Grey of Groby, eldest son of the Earl of Stamford, was nominated as major-general and commander-in-chief of all the forces raised in the association. Two days later, on 17 December, the commons resolved that Nottinghamshire should be asked to raise one hundred and fifty horse and four hundred foot for service in the North, to oppose the passage of the 'popish' army collecting under the Earl of Newcastle; and in the next few weeks the local parliamentary committee was empowered first to assess compulsorily all those who had not yet contributed to the raising of the county forces, and finally, to seize the rents, money, horses, plate and goods of all persons in arms for the king or giving voluntary help to his cause.

In Nottingham itself, while the negotiations with Newark were still proceeding, an appeal was issued on 18 December to

the gentry to join the citizens in the defence of the town, and it was resolved on the proposal of the committee to make two defensive gates at Chapel Bar and Cow Lane Bar, and to place a drawbridge on the bridge over the Leen across which the road from the south entered the town. A few days later, after Hutchinson's vain journey to meet the royalist agents, all negotiations for a treaty between the two hostile centres were dropped. Cavalier anxiety vanished with the appearance of Henderson and his men. The parliamentarians suspected after Hutchinson's experience that the projected treaty was merely a snare to gain time – and both sides, as the iron fingers of war fastened on the land, were impelled by forces they could no longer control. Sir John Gell sent some of his men to help in digging fortifications around Nottingham, volunteers came in from the countryside, and the three colonels who had earlier been named by parliament in the militia ordinance were asked to raise regiments.

Sir Francis Molyneux of Teversall declined, but Sir Francis Thornhagh agreed to raise a regiment of horse, and Francis Pierrepont undertook to provide a foot regiment. Thornhagh's regiment was commanded by his son Francis, whom he appointed to be its lieutenant-colonel. Ireton, who had been summoned back from Essex's army, was created major, his men being incorporated in the new regiment. Pierrepont persuaded John Hutchinson to accept the lieutenant-colonelcy of his foot, and he received his commission from Lord Grey on January 9, 1643. He had already raised one company, and his brother George, Gervase Lomax and one Scrimpshire recruited three other companies from among the townsmen. At the same time, the troop of dragoons which Charles White of Newthorpe had already enlisted on the western borders of the shire, was called back and occupied the castle.

So both sides organized and armed themselves, and in the few days between Christmas and the New Year the county was

engulfed in that dark shadow which was sweeping over the whole land. Newark and Nottingham became henceforth the focal points of the opposing causes in the shire, and it was in and around the two little towns that the main local struggle was fought out. The remainder of the county sent many of its gentry to fight for the king; it was obliged to pay heavy toll in money, provisions and horses to the successive armies which the shifting tide of war drove across its soil; and it was subjected more permanently either to the incessant demands of the parliamentary committees or to the plundering raids of the ubiquitous Newark horse. But it saw no fighting other than trivial skirmishes. Its towns like Retford, Worksop and Mansfield were open and unfortified, and the inhabitants appear to have bowed discreetly and of necessity to whichever party controlled their area for the time being. The more ardent spirits flocked up to the Yorkshire theatre of war or down to Newark or Nottingham; the less adventurous remained to endure as circumspectly as they could the burdens and the interruptions they were powerless to prevent.

The outbreak of war within the shire revealed at length the preponderant royalism of its nobility and gentry. Not a single peer, if we exclude the Earl of Rutland, who belonged rather to Leicestershire, declared for parliament, and only Clare vacillated. The remainder were solid in their support of Charles.

The Burning Bush

ROSEMARY ROBB

A present-day chronicler of East Midlands hauntings, Rosemary Robb tells this warming yet chilling tale in her 1992 book Ghost Hunting.

A certain vicar who once lived at nearby Goverton is still musing over a very strange experience he had one Christmas Eve. On the night in question the reverend gentleman had been taking Midnight Mass in St Peter's Church at Thurgarton, a church which was built on the site of the ancient Thurgarton Priory. He came out of the building around one o'clock in the morning after everyone had left, and started to drive along the lane from the priory towards the main road. Suddenly he slowed down. Something strange had caught his eye.

As he looked over to the left, where the ruins of the former chapter house of the priory are still visible, he could see the vivid glow of a burning bush. 'There was no doubt about it,' he said. 'But I remained in the car. Instinctively I knew that this was no ordinary fire.'

He later described it as an 'incandescent glow – like Moses and the burning bush – as distinct from something that had caught fire.'

All night he lay awake pondering over what he had seen. As soon as it was daylight he got into his car, anxious to return to the priory. He was determined to examine the spot where he had seen the vision.

To his amazement he could see no sign of fire where there should have been scorch marks. The ruins were still covered with weeds and grass as though nothing unusual had happened. Yet he knew he had not imagined it all.

The burning bush has never been seen again, but the tale was believed in the village. There is a local belief that it could have been the spirit of another clergyman who once carried out the ceremony of Midnight Mass many years ago.

Long Live the Guisers

MAURICE WILLIAM HOLMES

Maurice William Holmes of Underwood published this recollection of mumming or guising in Selston in 1992. The county has a rich tradition of mumming, much of it centred upon Plough Monday, early in the New Year – though as Christmas became more of a focal point of the year as the Victorian age progressed, the guisers began to realize that that was the best time for generous tips and the odd tipple on the house. These days there is a renewed interest in folk traditions, but when Mr Holmes and his colleagues were going through their paces in the late 1940s, there must have been times when they felt very much the last of a dying breed.

I became an actor during Christmas 1947, when I was thirteen years old. Up to this time I was so shy, so self-conscious, that I cringed every time I entered a cafe or room where people were present. But then I became a member of a group of guisers, sometimes called mummers, who went around Selston parish at Christmas, performing a kind of seasonal play that dates back to medieval times. Six boys with blackened faces formed the group.

The one who began the play was called the Opener In. Here one needed a lad full of gusto and self-confidence. In Keith Simpson we had just the right boy. Dressed in top hat and tails, he would knock loudly on the door of the house where we intended to perform, then walk straight in uninvited and begin. This element of surprise was vital, for once we were in, not many people stopped us – especially once their children saw Keith's blackened face. His opening lines were:

> I open the door and enter in,
> I beg your pardon to begin.
> Whether I sit or stand or fall
> I'll do my duty to please you all.
> Room, room, give us room
> To sport our merry rhyme,
> For remember, good sirs,
> 'Tis Christmastime.
> Step in, St George, and clear the way.

St George appeared, wielding a huge sword. Sometimes he would cut through any garlands that were hanging too low. Then he would shout:

> I am St George from Old England sprung,
> My name throughout the world has rung.

Many brave deeds and wonders have I known,
I have made tyrants tremble on their throne.
I followed a fair maid to dungeon deep,
Confounding beauty to meet her fate,
When a giant almost struck me dead,
But by my good valour I cut off his head.

After his noble speech I would run in dressed as a soldier and carrying a sword. My part was Slasher, and being disguised, I was able to give the part everything – all my inhibitions erased by soot and rouge. Confidently, I would begin:

I am a gallant soldier and Slasher is my name,
With sword and buckler by my side
I'm sure to win the game.
A fight with thee, St George, if thou art able,
Disable, disable, stand thee not in my power
For if I draw my glistening sword
I'll soon thee devour.
My arms of brass, my body of steel
No man on earth can make me feel.

St George would then challenge me to a fight, waving his sword in my face shouting:

Stand back. Stand back thou dirty dog.
I'll make your buttons fly.
I'll cut thy belly clean in two
And thou will surely die.
Take guard, you white-livered beast
For hungry crows on you will feast.

I would begin to fight St George; then, after about half a minute, I would fall on the floor, seriously wounded. Then

Keith, the Opener In, would shout:

A doctor. A doctor. Ten pounds for a doctor.

A boy dressed as a doctor would run in carrying a black bag. He would say:

I am a doctor, sir.
Opener: Art thou really a doctor, sir?
Doctor: Yes, sir, I am.
Opener: Italy, Sicily, France and Spain,
O'er the seas and home again.
What can'st thou cure?
Doctor: The itch, the stitch, the palsy and gout,
If there were nineteen devils in I'd cast
twenty out.
Opener: Then cure me this man.

The doctor would then kneel beside Slasher, take a bottle from his bag and proceed to administer the potion, saying:

Here, Jack, take a little nip-nap
And shove it down thy tip-tap
And live to fight again.

I would rise again, and the four of us would stand back as Beelzebub entered, carrying a club and a dripping pan. He would say:

In comes our old Beelzebub,
Over me shoulder I carries me club,
In me hand a dripping pan,
Don't you think I'm a jolly old man?
If you don't, I do.

Bad finger, battered bag – it can only be the Doctor in the mumming play.

Now if you think I'm a fool
And got no sense,
Put your hands in your pockets
And gis a few pence.

Beelzebub moved over and stood with the others as he held out the dripping pan. Then Devildoubt appeared, carrying a sweeping brush and saying:

In comes little Devildoubt
With his breeches inside out,
Money I want and money I crave,
If you don't give me money
I'll sweep you to the grave.

Devildoubt then began to sweep the floor, and all the players began to sing a carol before Beelzebub took the pan around

The Theatre Royal in Nottingham, home of festive entertainment rather more professionally presented than the guisers' shows.

for the collection. Mostly we would be given a shilling, sometimes more, depending on people's generosity. Occasionally we would enter redolent, dimly-lit kitchens without the lady of the house hearing us; then, if she appeared, she would become spellbound or hysterical on seeing our black faces. Sometimes while the Opener In was performing, we would stand patiently waiting in the kitchen; likely as not a mince pie or two would stray into our hands. If we were lucky, the landlord of the village pub would let us perform there. This would be our bonanza, for after our play came the great collection – and mostly people give more when under the influence. There was one drawback, though: when the doctor gave me the potion there was always some wag ready virtually to pour his ale down my throat. One Christmas, after playing at the Red Lion and two rooms of the Miners' Welfare, I finished up more like a drunken soldier than a gallant one.

Most of us came from poor families, and we earned more money this way than we had ever had before – but it was tough work, especially in the harsh winters of 1946 and 1947. I remember how our feet became anaesthetized, our ears stinging with the biting frosts. As we plodded through the snow, the shivering wires overhead became our garlands, the swan-necked street lamps our fairy lights.

One Christmas Eve we decided to ask the local mine owner, who lived in a big house about half a mile away from the village. 'We should make at least a pound there,' said Keith. So off we trudged up the hill, past the farm with its sugar-loaf haystack, past the meadows shining lake-like in the moonlight, then on to the rich man's house, which was set in an acre of grounds. On arriving, we crunched our way under the stone arch with its icy coping and scrambled to be first to bang the heavy lion's head door-knocker. I can still recall how startled the butler looked when he saw our blackened faces and fancy dress. Then we became startled as two huge

Thank goodness today's generation can still find fun in winter pursuits enjoyed by their grandparents.

bloodhounds appeared, snarling ferociously and fixing us with glassy-eyed stares.

After we had explained our business, we were kindly invited to perform for the kitchen staff while the butler went to enquire if the master would allow us to act before his family. Twenty minutes later, our appetites sated and five precious shillings clutched tightly in Keith's hand, we were ushered along a dimly-lit passage, flanked by suits of armour and dark period furniture. Eventually, we were given the cue to begin. When it was my turn, I distinctly remember noticing the vastness of the room, and feeling the warmth emanating from its big ornamental fireplace. I also remember that as I lay wounded, my face was only inches away from the toothy end of a tigerskin rug. The children of the house, who had

obviously never seen the likes of us before, loved the performance and clapped rapturously. After the applause, we waited confidently for what we all thought would be a large reward. It was fortunate that our expressions were hidden behind greasepaint as the moustachioed, tweed-coated master of the house handed Keith two florins, saying smugly:

'Jolly good show, lads. You must come and entertain us again next year.'

As we walked away from the tight-fisted affluence, we vowed we would never again return to that particular residence.

Acknowledgements

An extract from *George, Memoirs of a Gentleman's Gentleman*, by Nina Slingsby Smith, published by Jonathan Cape, 1984, is reprinted by permission of Random House UK Ltd. 'Christmas in Florence, 1926', by D.H. Lawrence, an extract from *The Letters of D.H. Lawrence*, vol. 5, published by Cambridge University Press, is reprinted with acknowledgements to Laurence Pollinger Ltd and the estate of Frieda Lawrence Ravagli. 'A Christmas Party, 1900', an extract from *The Pavior* magazine, September 1955, and *High Pavement Remembered, 1788–1988*, edited by Alan Bates, both published by High Pavement College, Bestwood, Nottingham, is reprinted with acknowledgements to the college. 'Snowstorm of Christmas Day, 1836' is an extract from *Recollections of Old Nottingham*, by Mrs A. Gilbert, published by H.B. Saxton, Nottingham, 1904. An extract from *Two of Clubs*, by Joan Wallace, Gowan Publishing Ltd, Nottingham, 1985, is reprinted by permission of the author. An extract from *Never Let Anyone Draw the Blinds*, by Lottie Martin, edited by Julie O'Neill, published by Paula Hill, Wollaton, is reprinted with acknowledgements to the copyright holders. An extract from *Victorian Worksop*, by Michael J. Jackson, published by the Worksop Archaeological and Local History Society, 1992, is reprinted by permission of the author. 'A Christmas Hamper, 1895' is by John Hudson from newspaper cuttings. 'Christmas in the Trenches' consists of extracts from *The Robin Hoods, 1914–18*, by officers of the regiment, published by J. & H. Bell Ltd, Nottingham, 1921. 'Christmas, 1965' is by John Hudson from newspaper cuttings. An extract from *Georgian Southwell*, edited by R.E. Hardstaff and Philip Lyth, financed by Newark and Sherwood District Council, is reprinted by permission of R.E. Hardstaff and Newark and Sherwood District Council. 'The Christmas Treadmill' is an extract from *Observations on Prison Discipline*, by Benjamin Hutchinson, published by S. & J. Ridge, Newark, 1823. '1814: The Thirteen Week Frost', an extract from *The Derbyshire and Nottinghamshire Weather Book*, by Len Markham, published by Countryside Books, Newbury, 1994, is reprinted by permission of the copyright holders. Four extracts from *The Owl*, Nottingham, 4 January 1878. An extract from *Life of a Country Boy, 1925–1940*, by Victor Smyth,

published by the author, 1993, is reprinted by permission of the author. 'Bring Four of Your Thieves' is by John Hudson. 'Garth Hepplewhite's Come-uppance', by Ambrose Gadd, first published under the title 'The Diary of a Stroller' in the *Nottingham Observer*, December 1957, is reprinted with acknowledgements to the copyright holders. An extract from *It's Trew Worram Tellin' Yer*, edited by Mike Wilkinson and others of the Sutton-in-Ashfield Living Memories Group, this extract by Anne Spencer, is reprinted by permission of the copyright holders. 'Robin Hood and his Little Friends' was first published in *Playbox Annual*, 1924. 'Riot at the Soup House', an extract from *The Diary of Abigail Gawthern of Nottingham, 1751–1810*, edited by Adrian Henstock, first published in the Thoroton Society Record Series, vol. 33, 1980, is reprinted by permission of the author and the society. 'Poor Owd 'Oss', an extract from *Legends of Nottinghamshire*, by Pat Mayfield, published by Dalesman, Clapham, Lancaster, 1976, is reprinted with acknowledgements to the copyright holders. 'The Pilgrims' First Christmas' is an extract from *The Pilgrims and their History*, by Roland G. Usher, Macmillan, New York, 1918. 'Signs of Trouble', an extract from *Walking the Beat with Albert RN, Book 2*, by Albert Walker, published by the author through Newark Chamber of Commerce, 1990, is reprinted by permission of the author. 'Christmas at the Workhouse', by One Who Has Seen Better Days, was first published in *The Owl*, Nottingham, 25 December 1886. An extract from *The Man Who Worked On Sundays*, by the Revd Leslie Skinner, published by the author, is reprinted with acknowledgements to the copyright holders. 'Christmas Seventy Years Ago', an extract from *Neville Bingham's Trilogy, Memoirs of Sutton-on-Trent*, by Neville Bingham, published 1991, is reprinted by permission of Nick Bingham and Sally Glover. 'Yuletide in Bygone Days', an extract from *Quaint Lore of Nottinghamshire*, by S. Jackson Coleman, published by the Folklore Fellowship, is reprinted with acknowledgements to the copyright holders. 'Death at Christmas', an extract from *Personal Copy*, by Ray Gosling, published by Faber and Faber, 1980, is reprinted with acknowledgements to the copyright holders. 'Doles and Confects' is an extract from *Notes About Notts*, edited by Cornelius Brown, published by T. Forman & Sons, Long Row, Nottingham, 1874. 'Storm Clouds of War', an extract from *Nottinghamshire in the Civil War*, by Alfred C. Wood, Clarendon Press, 1937, is reprinted with acknowledgements to the copyright holders. 'The Burning Bush', an extract from *Ghost Hunting*, by Rosemary Robb, published by J.H. Hall & Sons, Derby, 1992, is reprinted with acknowledgements to the author. 'Long Live the Guisers', an extract from *Old*

Nottingham Remembered, by Maurice William Holmes, published 1992, is reprinted with acknowledgements to the copyright holders.

Thanks are due to the staff of the local studies department, Nottingham Central Library, and the reference department, Newark Library; and especially, for help in production, to Jane Calvert of France Lynch, near Stroud.

Picture Credits

Pictures are from the author's collection except various press cuttings and: page 17, Gowan Publishing Ltd; page 20, Robert Opie Collection, Gloucester; pages 29, 59, 79, 86, 140, 143, Bristol United Press; pages 48, 51, 97, 102, Nottingham Historical Film Unit; page 94, Newark Chamber of Commerce, Printing and Graphic Design Department; pages 110, 114, Boots, Nottingham.